Towards a Canada of Light

BY B.W. POWE

BOOKS

A Climate Charged
The Solitary Outlaw
A Tremendous Canada of Light
Outage
The Unsaid Passing

EDITOR

Light Onwords/Light Onwards—The Living Literacies Record

CD-ROM

"Noise of Time," in The Glenn Gould Profile

EVENTS

Marshall McLuhan: What If He Was Right?, York University, 1997
The Trudeau Era, York University, 1998
Living Literacies, York University, 2002

TOWARDS A
CANADA *of* LIGHT

B. W. POWE

Thomas Allen Publishers
Toronto

Library and Archives Canada Cataloguing in Publication

Powe, B. W. (Bruce W.), 1955–
Towards a Canada of light / B. W. Powe.

Previously pub. under titles: A Canada of light, and A tremendous Canada of light.
ISBN-13: 978-0-88762-228-1
ISBN-10: 0-88762-228-3

1. Canada–Politics and government. 2. Canada–Civilization.
3. Communication–Canada. I. Powe, B. W. (Bruce W.), 1955– Canada of light.
II. Powe, B. W. (Bruce W.), 1955– Tremendous Canada of light. III. Title.

FC630.P69 2006   971   C2006-902844-3

Editor: Patrick Crean
Jacket and text design: Gordon Robertson
Cover image: First Light

Published by Thomas Allen Publishers,
a division of Thomas Allen & Son Limited,
145 Front Street East, Suite 209,
Toronto, Ontario M5A 1E3 Canada

www.thomas-allen.com

Originally published in 1993 by Coach House Press, Toronto.
Previous paperback edition published in 1997
by Somerville House Books, Toronto.

  Canada Council for the Arts

The publisher gratefully acknowledges the support of
The Ontario Arts Council for its publishing program.

We acknowledge the support of the Canada Council for the Arts, which last year invested $20.0 million in writing and publishing throughout Canada.

We acknowledge the Government of Ontario through the Ontario Media Development Corporation's Ontario Book Initiative.

We acknowledge the financial support of the Government of Canada through the Book Publishing Industry Development Program (BPIDP) for our publishing activities.

10 09 08 07 06   1 2 3 4 5

Printed and bound in Canada

For my children

. . . and my eyes followed the spin of the fields newly laid out for sowing, the oak woods with hard bronze survivor leaves, and a world of great size beyond, or fair clouds and then of abstraction, a tremendous Canada of Light.

—SAUL BELLOW, *The Adventures of Augie March*

Contents

A Prayer for Canada

A NEW INTRODUCTION

I wrote this book to counter the mood in my country. That was one of my many motives—one of the reasons behind the inception of its spirit. What was that mood? It was the powerful feeling, wrenching really, that there was a dead-end sign at the turn of what should have been a wide thoroughfare. It was the feeling, strong in the night, dogging me during the day, that the circuits were being blocked when energy, a great free sweep, should have been flowing through, flowing on. The writing of this book came from a sense, haunting, at times hazing, that politicians' words were swords blindly used: cutting people, separating us from our higher selves, dividing us from one another, driving cultures into an atmosphere of perpetual war. I also had the sense that the corporatist directives of slashing and firing were meant for the few who accepted it was best to do without an elusive, unquantifiable factor, like heart.

Canada, this name, this place: what I was feeling, intimately, as if she were a part of me, not a mere country where I happened to be born and that often felt like my home. I found myself sometimes drawing maps of her on scraps of paper. And when I did, the mood came over me again: a force was seizing her, closing down the feel of wide fresh space, wild mind and imagination, potential and welcoming, where you could dream, and hear the angles of many voices, see vistas that said, Build and be what you can. I kept hearing the words "restriction" and "prohibition," "limitation" and "narrowing," instead of words like "audacity" and "breathing freely." That seizure was like a choking sensation. A power was pressing the life out of a country. I thought then, and still think, that one way to push back at this force that threatens to close off your capacity for reverie, to imagine, to sing out with sheer pleasure, to redirect yourself towards the stars, and to love intensely what comes to you, is to make your language soar into blockades and barriers, bringing them down—slowly, patiently—with the energy of enwombing words. Find the peak of your spiritual power in words, and you could begin to break through.

And yet why does such language embarrass us? Why does visionary language seem impossible now, so subject to contempt? It's perhaps too vulnerable to misinterpretation, too elliptically poetic—certainly lacking in the requisite withering doubt; and certainly not in keeping with the prevailing cynicism, the acceptable hard-heartedness, which you find masquerading behind the phrase "being realistic." "Back to reality," people say when they give up a vacation, return to drudgery, working in situations they secretly despise, returning to a reality that has been established and coordinated by someone else. The beginning of tyranny, William Blake never tired of articulating in his prophetic poems, is always in the levelling of single vision. What is single vision? The imposition of one way of seeing things, and subsequently the belief that there is only one way of being: so when a society and a culture, a political system and an economic model, begin to appear uniform in their power and effect, people feel that narrowing in their lives, as if their voices are being cut off, their avenues of travel blocked. We become slaves the moment we hand the keys to the definitions of reality entirely over to someone else, whether it is a business, an economic theory, a political party, the White House, Newsworld or CNN. If we succumb to single vision, so Blake said, to someone's way of perceiving (forms of propaganda, whatever side delivers it), then we fall, and fall asleep, slaves then to whatever system sets the coordinates for the discussion. Democracies should be a delirium of choices—more options, not fewer; more avenues to travel, not fewer. If we are to take the idea of liberty seriously—and I'm not convinced that some people do: the terror of being alive, of having to choose a destiny every day, at almost every moment, is too overwhelming—then surely we must recognize that the democratic essence is an abundance of original spirit and imagination. More of the mosaic, then, and less of the melting pot: more of the plurality of peoples and languages and faiths and attitudes and conversations, and less assimilation. The agent of the new is kept alive by interpretation, more additions to the mosaic, by extending and broadening the range of reception, and of perception. *A Canada of Light* was dedicated to the encouraging, the heartening, of the idea that this quietly extravagant experiment in many ideas and languages expresses an energy that upsets any attempt at single vision. Canada's lightness of spirit means free play: a bearable lightness, agility in the changing currents, never to be loaded down by a past of racial hatred, by aggressive dogmatism, ancient acrimonies or grievances, the zealotry of an immutable idea of what a state should be.

This book has undergone transformations. That has primarily been because of changes in the circumstances in which I took up the subject again.

I wrote the first version, in 1992, in a euphoria of births. The twins, Katie and Thomas, had arrived. They were only months old when I began writing. It was my intention to give them a packet full of promises and faith. And I wanted to tell them about what dreams and futures their country could embrace—why their father loved being here, what love could be passed on. Where was I, then, when I wrote that edition? All I can say for certain, I thought I was elsewhere when the words came. Now I'm likely to say that place was, simply, hope.

The second version, revised and enlarged in 1996, came from a less euphoric time. Harsh divorce proceedings were on my mind. The twins were spending time divided—weeks in one home, then weeks in another: our lives scattered. Still I had to telegraph glimmers greater than our strained circumstance. I wanted to give them a view of their country's illuminating beauty. In that revision I was not only reminding my children of the energies thriving around us, and in us, but also trying to remind myself of that availability and abundance.

This third version was reconsidered, and redirected, in 2005, after September 11, 2001, after wars, and the morass for American soldiers and politicians in Iraq. One of those wars involves a considerable deployment of Canadian troops in Afghanistan. My children, almost teenagers, grow accustomed to news of terrorist bombings, of gunfights flaring in the streets of Toronto. This is assuming that one ever truly becomes accustomed to such news. People have said, How would you write this book now? What would you say to a world possessed by terrorism and war, where the language of budget slashing has been replaced by the grimmer dictations of security?

Surely the fight is still to overcome dead-end states of mind that seek to confine imagination and spirit. There is a joke going around the circuit: Canadians don't need a national dream, they are already awake. This is true only to a certain extent, if we see dreaming purely in terms of delusion, and dreams solely in contrast to a so-called "reality principle," which usually means confining discussions to questions of material existence. The Aboriginal people speak of dreaming true, Gaston Bachelard wrote of the necessity of dreaming well: reverie yields to self-agency—and to imaginings that, in Northrop Frye's definition of imagination, can open to tolerance, sympathy, the creation of more beginnings (opportunities, options), the re creation of more stories (enlarging consciousness to an infinity of infusing worlds), the refusal to accept definitions of reality that contain us, or trap us.

Writing the first version quickly, in a mere six weeks, I felt then, and feel now, that it was given to me. Some books are brutally hard work—tough slogging through every word choice and sentence arrangement. Other books are offerings, easing through you in a way that seems like a gracious

entrancement. Though I've subsequently rearranged para-
graphs and sections, and expanded on phrases and refined
sentences, to make it reverberate more with different states
of mind, the core of it, the gift if its ease—to express my love
for Canada's unfolding destiny, the spark that quixotically
flashes—hasn't changed. I keep playing with the book, redis-
covering it, then leaving it in an unfinished state, because
I've come to believe that this is my homage to Canada: a perpetually unfinished book for a country that refuses to make
sense to anyone: an evolving book (different in every appearance) to evoke the counter-country that can't and won't freeze
into any one mask. A counter-country? . . . Not against or
above nationhood, but an experiment, running counter to
expectation, counter to the idea of empire. In this book I felt
that I gave myself permission to wander, and so the writing
took on a life of its own and chafed against restriction and
limitation by insisting on ambivalence and intuition, resist-
ing uniformity and polished completion, relishing the elusive
and fragmentary. I'm fascinated by elusiveness. The lack of
resolution, the unsolved—they trace the questionings that
inform our beginnings: "What if . . . ?" "Who speaks . . . ?"
"Where are you going . . . ?" "Where is here . . . ?" If there is
anything I've learned from *A Canada of Light* it is to live in
questions, love the questions.

   Nevertheless, it bears the marks of the times when it was
written. The references to Prime Minister Brian Mulroney's
economic policies, and to the referendum held on the Charlottetown Accord, belong to the mid- and late 1980s and the
early 1990s. I've changed several specific references, and made

the address to the powers that be more to the rulers whose faces and forms change but whose sway continues. Parts of this work belong to the past. To honour those moments, I've let some of them be.

———

What has changed in a devastating way is our relationship to a militarized America. After 9/11, the Patriot Act, the advent of Homeland Security, the suspension of civil rights for suspected terrorists and non-combatants, the exporting of suspects without lawyer or trial to countries that sanction torture, Canada seems more like Athens, cerebral and contemplative, during the time of Sparta. It is as if our culture and politics have been reincarnated from that model of the chattering, philosophical state set alongside the society efficiently organized for action—one, and only one, purpose: the idealized crusade of its wars.

The contexts and conditions of power do shift. The watchwords in other decades were "debt . . . credit ratings . . . deficit cutting . . . balanced budgeting . . ." While these continue to have momentum, the watchwords after 9/11 have become "war . . . terror . . . security . . . sacrifice . . . patriotism . . ."

Always look to the impressive mood of your time, its flooding sensations—the informing images and the icons in the headlines and clichés, the advertising and commercials, new technologies and the way they are being put to use—to approach the groundwork of structural articulation. Marshall McLuhan said such a descent into the maelstrom must be done with contemplative stillness and suspended judgment. But, so McLuhan knew, nothing is that clear and simple. The storm alters the perceiver: the perceiver's mind and sensibility alter the interpretation of the storm.

Contemplate what it means for Canada to be ethereal Athens during the time of Spartan supremacy. In Sparta an entire society became a highly disciplined war machine, cast in a self-image of innocence. War was noble self-sacrifice, a duty performed for the idealist cause, which was the community of stabilizing, imperishable castes. They maintained a rock-solid theology of fearsome gods who would aid them in the devouring of opposition to their ideal. Once attacked, Sparta unified hurriedly, organizing vast storehouses of wealth, wrapping itself in the mantle of unassailable virtue, under the leadership of a ruthless elite who insisted they knew what was right. The warriors invaded others with little hesitation. They carried their weapons into their homes, into the markets, for threats and danger lurked everywhere. Plato grudgingly admired the sober, militarist communalism of the Spartans—parts of *The Republic*, and his commentary in the *Laws*, were likely modelled on the clarity and idealism that community embodied around a single idea: its conviction of moral superiority.

America has turned Spartan. Their virtues are praised, hardness, coldness. War is the great enterprise, the military the great heroes. Its concepts of liberty and piety must prevail. People outside its borders are potential invaders. Even its neighbouring allies are most probably havens, harbouring cells. We have every reason to fear this brand of crusading idealism. America is no longer a temporarily armed camp: it is a fully militarized society, whose economy and politics meld in its aims, which is the subordination of others to their sense of insecurity. While post 9/11 Americans are radically divided between the puritan imperium and the dissent tradition—the transcendentalist spirit of Ralph Waldo Emerson, Henry David Thoreau, Walt Whitman and Harriet Beecher Stowe, a spirit continually reborn and renewed in Henry Miller, Allen Ginsberg, Susan Sontag, Norman Mailer and Gore Vidal—Canadians are perched on the empire's edge. Margins are usually good places to be. They offer observation posts, cusps for reflection. But at the moment living directly beside a well-fenced society, whose evangelists proudly proclaim that God is on their side, leaves Canadians dauntingly vulnerable. Sparta stirs again, with the capability of turning on its own. Its allies often recoil, but live on tenterhooks. And what can we do when we have handed most defence measures to the Spartans? Residing beside an unequivocal and determined order will be difficult for those who prize evasive complexity and messy ambivalence. Some on the margin of the empire will come to admire the lucid will and force of the warriors' iron resolve. Such a commanding organization should elicit our respect; but joining up with the militarization is another matter. Nor should America's turn towards Spartan idealism be a cause for smug condemnation. It must be of profound concern to us, because America has carried the torch of liberty too: yet in the name of liberty, we see liberty curtailed, and the forces of probation and restriction given absolute authority, gaining ground and strength.

All is not uniform in America, fortunately. In few other places do we find more trenchant critiques of the militarization of the United States than among Americans themselves. Here is Tony Judt's pained summary of the Spartan ascendancy from his essay, ironically titled "The New World Order" (*The New York Review of Books,* July 14, 2005)

Why does the US Department of Defense currently maintain 725 official military bases outside the country and 969 at home (not to mention numerous secret bases)? Why does the US spend more on "defense" than all the rest of the world put together? After all, it has no present or likely enemies of the kind who could be intimidated or defeated by "star wars" missile defense or bunker-busting "nukes." And yet this country is obsessed with war: rumors of war, images of war, "preemptive" war, "preventive" war, "surgical" war, "prophylactic" war, "permanent" war. As President Bush explained at a news conference on April 13, 2004, "This country must go on the offense and stay on the offense." . . . Among democracies, only in America do soldiers and other uniformed servicemen figure ubiquitously in political photo ops and popular movies. Only in America do civilians eagerly buy expensive military service vehicles for suburban shopping runs. In a country no longer supreme in most other fields of human endeavour, war and warriors have become the last, enduring symbols of American dominance and the American way of life. "In war, it seemed," writes [Andrew J.] Bacevich, "lay America's true comparative advantage." . . . In a militarized society the range of acceptable opinion inevitably shrinks. Opposition to the "commander in chief" is swiftly characterized as *lèse-majesté*; criticism becomes betrayal. No nation, as Madison wrote in 1795 and Bacevich recalls approvingly, can "preserve its freedom in the midst of continual warfare." "Full-spectrum dominance" begins as a Pentagon cliché and ends as an executive project. . . . The international anarchy so painstakingly averted by two generations of enlightened American statesmen may soon engulf us again. President Bush sees "freedom" on the march. I wish I shared his optimism. I see a bad moon rising.

The origin of corruption in politics is surely in the thought that you are the bearer of ultimate virtue. Nothing more effectively corrupts than the idea that you act purely on behalf of the ideal state. Further, that so many books and essays, reports and editorials, movies and TV programming are now devoted to the ethics of torture and imprisonment—when it is permissible, when it is not—and that so many voices give authority and approval to the military interpretation of reality, must reveal how far terror has penetrated into the psyche.

America, you teem with nightmares, after the falling towers. Canadians, and the Athenian soul living north of the future, flinch in shock, but also in dismay at the military society that publicly prizes its own virtue. The philosophical spirit is the only domain of originality left to a country that has shorn itself of economic and military independence. That spirit, however, knows it is ethical and imaginative to swerve and bend. *Rigor mortis* is the one thing you can count on to be hard and immovable.

Who will say where future generations will look for light? Towards Sparta reborn? Towards the brief glimmer of Athens? And, yes (lest we forget), in Athens—devoted to excellence (though more often in sports than in ideas) and the cultivation of the *polis* where eloquent points of view could flourish—the rulers ordered Socrates to commit suicide. Nor should we forget that Athens had slaves. Yet our last liberty, that of the spirit, of mind, is considerable, not to be underestimated. Our counter, then: the prizing of the original spark in each, keeping thought bold, our mental landscapes a frontier. Athens becomes Canada, where ranges of race and thought and custom and voice marry, and inward domains and destinies intersect.

Why not sing Canada? Why is it unseemly to do so? We have our visionary, transcendental tradition, beginning truly with Richard Maurice Bucke's *Cosmic Consciousness* in 1904—a work influenced by the itinerant Whitman, who befriended Bucke—and its subterranean influence on McLuhan. He quotes, suggestively, and approvingly, Bucke's phrase, "cosmic consciousness," in his chapter, "The Spoken Word," in *Understanding Media*. The global village vision burst on the mind of the mantic philosopher who chose to live here and nowhere else. Frye thought Canada was "the eternal borderline," embodying a destiny to be a home for the world's interpreters, where readers could deepen their levels of comprehension and so enlarge their tolerance for differing modes of perception. Contemplation and interpretation through education—itself another form of quest, of honing inner destiny—wouldn't leave much time for anyone to become violent.

Canada has a garrison mentality, Frye said slyly. This meant we would have to rely on the creation of verbal universes to push back, through variegated imaginative expression, the heavier, determined concentrations of propaganda and clichés. The garrison is an outpost for the imagination. Thus it would appear to be a jail or fortress to those stuck in seeing power only through the lens of political economy. McLuhan's paradoxical insight was that the lack of a Canadian identity was our identity. This speaks of flexibility too, and of the knowledge that identity is enigmatic. Canada was the Distant Early Warning Line for McLuhan (space gridded by electrical sources) where you could (paradoxically, again) slow down, plead for the time to contemplate and chronicle, and satirize and laugh. Laughter also wouldn't leave time for anyone to be self-righteously or mindlessly violent. Pierre Trudeau brought us the Constitution and Charter to give broad outline to what has become an evolving and sophisticated culture of rights. He spoke to us whenever he could in the language of destiny, which is the language of eminence: we could aspire to living in a just society, if we were willing to acknowledge that Canadians would have to swerve away from systems of power based on precedents established by others. Our experiment was emerging at the right moment, and it didn't have to follow the American model, nor the British and the European.

And there is the singing voice every Canadian knows, through the cool wind that rustles down from the north, through the trees that have come to resemble Tom Thomson's brush strokes. Perhaps our national emblem should be the whole tree, not just a turning leaf: the red pine that shows it can lean into the west wind. But it should be the tree turned upside down. The mystic tree of life in the kabbalah has its roots in the air and its spreading branches and growing leaves in the earth, emblems of ever-deepening complexity.

I wrote this—another motive—to find the way to sing somehow (though my children will attest to the fact that I can't carry a tune) through the country's air, and of the country's breadth and breath. Sometimes you need to let your soul sing—"clap its hands and sing," said William Butler Yeats in *Sailing to Byzantium*—even if you can't actually do so, when the shadows are large enough to black out the light. If we listen hard enough, we may hear the wind rush and its whisper, "Where I please . . ." Which means you are free to choose the forms you will serve, free to find what will serve you, free to follow your fascination (if you wish to follow anything at all), free to choose what will seed and root you. If something is in the wind then it is always about to happen. Moreover, if something is in the wind then it can also blow away, leaving only a trace or a hint in the dust, like the spirit that is supposed to live between the letters.

All of this is why I find Canada beautiful.

None of these reflections answer, in any definitive formula, the question I've been asked: How would you write this book now? The reflections no doubt don't form a basis for policy. They are responses, nevertheless. And when there are more responses, perhaps there will be more beginnings. I put questions back to others: If Canada fails, what hope has the rest of the embattled and battling world? And if we are challenged for our cultural survival, on what grounds will we fight, if that challenge is not to be military?

However, we must recognize the weight of darkness—the blunt trauma of dead ends. Call these the shadows or blockages that abide. Two of my colleagues, Jane Jacobs and Ronald Wright, in pessimistic moods, said in their recent, admirable books (*Dark Age Ahead, A Short History of Progress*) that darkness looms. They argue that barbarism will descend from ignorance and social breakdown, the exhaustion of natural resources, the stretching to the limit of healthcare facilities, the lack of faith in democratic processes, the seductions of extremism. This darkness is already here. It has been so for a long time, perhaps for an aeon. It is found in the politics of unending war: it is found in the shooters and wandering youths who have nothing in their eyes, not even despair: it is found in the economics that continues to keep a good portion of the world impoverished: it is found in our addictions to bad news, to being enthralled by the eyes of the killers who appear on TV screens: it is found in the fanaticism that holds an allure because of its determined, pious clarity: it is found in any teaching that tells you that your life will be meaningless, as if you have been lifted out of a river speckled with light and set down on a muddy bank, where you have been told to wait or do nothing: it is found in the cynicism and smarminess of knowing commentators: it is found in the denial experts coolly provide when they say we are not responsible for poisoning our planet: it is found in terrorist bombings and the shuddering recognition that there will be more. Yet individual lives do ignite with light. The generation of the young, the time of my children and of the students I encounter, has been called indigo—no longer Generation X or Y (a colour being preferable to a letter?)—because so many of their souls seem cast in an eerie blue radiance: what you see in the promise in their eyes, the vibration of their eagerness and health, something greater about to come. They are, to paraphrase Rainer Maria Rilke, the doctors who must watch over themselves.

But Jacobs and Wright are accurate to some extent: darkness has been descending over the last centuries. Fear remains a block, murderousness a weight. Empty cynicism and apathy, exploitation and manipulation hammer the soul. We smash into the looming shadows, like canoeists on a black-night river suddenly running up against an unmapped towering rock, and we wonder, What is our way around? Still there are people who insist on the spark that is in us, sometimes flickering, sometimes fading. The best one can do is to fan the sparks, and hope the glow will continue to rise against the roll of darkness.

One of the sparks is the place I want to evoke and summon in these pages: a Canada of light, a promise, a flash, an opportunity for reverie, a turning leaf, an opened door, a rendezvous of many cultures, a sometimes quieter street or pathway in the wailing world, an outpost, a DEW Line, the least likely place to incite mass ethnic hatred, a glimpse, a turning away, a provocation to think beyond single vision, a drama of inwardness, a site for talk and contemplations, a celebration of solitudes, a generous spirit wrestling with the demon of closure and the shadow of uniformity, where the vision of the country remains, fortunately, always ahead of its politicians. Gather depth and expanse, and patiently come together in the night to know beauty. Deepen solitudes, and love the unsolved. Salute each other across the truest eternal border-line, which is not national, but human.

Thus is my prayer.

Maxims and Enigmas

The old Canada has ended. Nothing fully formed has emerged in the raw, agitated state. Blurred lives, overwhelmed minds, lost souls, thwarted spirit—these appear to be our bequest. Yet we start, and live, moving in all directions at once because we are driven to do so.

———————

In the rampage of what seems to be terminal disagreements and divisions, rising confusions and intolerance, we can be certain of this: our time and place have been electrified.

———————

Electricity sparks, clings, searching for conductors and channels to illuminate, to jolt. It is the life-energy concentrated in wires, across airwaves. Wherever such energies criss-cross, or intersect, finding outlets, they bring cords and discords— harmonies and alliances, turmoil and noise. Our amplifiers, or electronic technologies, heighten the perpetual shifting that is living itself, making rampant change our exhilarating, harrowing circumstance.

———————

Electricity alters our relationship with every social contract by speeding up and intensifying our engagements and experiences. We live squeezed, accelerated—images and pictures and voices and sounds pouring all at once, surging at every moment. Questions burst upon us: What is citizenship in this condition when information hurtles at us? How do we remain individuals who can make choices and influence systems and institutions in the mass technological milieu? What is the role of government in the borderless atmosphere? Where are our boundary lines? How do we stay responsive—alive and not yet numbed, souls not yet diminished or shrunken by exposure to too much stuff, too many competing images and voices?

———————

I am more and more moved by the question of what kind of political state we will choose when commerce and computers combine to launch and support a borderless economic world order. Must politics be divorced from questions of the humane spirit, of justice? Are there alternative currents to the emergence of a single state obsessed by security and capital?

Magnetism generates fields, electricity enhances flow. Electromagnetism melds field and flow in startling arrangements of attraction and repulsion. One of the alternative currents, and arrangements, is a Canada of light.

This light state is where history dances lightly. What I mean by lightness is the dancer's light step: lightness opposed to heaviness or weight, lightness opposed to tragedy and gloom, to traumatized and paralyzing experience. According to physicists, in quantum mechanics and relativity theory, we are ourselves made of light and energy, beings who share in the particles and events of planets and moons, comets and stars.

I'm referring here to a state of light-in-the soul, a lightness of spirit that we can find in a country, which continues to exist in striking contrast to other societies. This light state is where the wired world plays out one possible myth I find exemplary for our anguished, wrangling world. If only we could breathe in the lightness—learn how to let it lift us forward.

Blaise Pascal wrote, "Nothing stands still for us." Firm groundings, unmovable positions, are delusions, even dangerous, because we roll on waves of unknown depth and extent: we are vulnerable to torrents and tides. Every seemingly fixed point must shift. Yet we often burn with the desire to find what could be lasting.

We have added to this recognition that life is a question, a passionate quest. Global mayhem stuns us, rioting on an unprecedented scale—those amplifiers, the electronic media, deepen our consciousness of others and their demands, thus

expanding experience, and sometimes searing and shearing
our senses with rages of emotion. Mass technologies hook us
into the fundamental fields and currents of the universe: the
wired and wireless machines accelerate and alter natural flux.
We have created a machine-state that mirrors us and exposes
us, and yet can alienate us from the world, and from one
another. In a terminal flash, electricity jumps up contraries
and contradictions. William Blake's *The Marriage of Heaven
and Hell* is an everyday occurrence: surrealism is the pulse of
the streets. Ovid's *Metamorphosis* is the stuff of reality: we are
hurried through Dante's *Divine Comedy* at night through
our TV screens, but without a Virgil to guide us and without
Beatrice's promised blessing at the end. The implicit contradictions in minds and souls are rendered explicit at every
turn by the electronic screening and exposure. Cubism and
pluralism are no longer an art movement and a political
theory: they are facts, what we engage daily.

So we plug into electric currents and fields without tuning
ourselves, providing our psyches and sensibilities with insu-
lation, the refinements of learning: arduous self-knowledge.
Out of tune we will spin: but in tune, we could dance.

Here is the story of the word "electric." It comes from the
Latin *electrum*, meaning amber, a fossil resin that exhibits

electrical power when rubbed, and from a Greek root word, meaning "a gleaming." Electricity occurs when energy poles between two objects of friction. That friction leads to sparks of light, and to the paradox that light can be both a wave and a field. And we need light to make our way, and see our destiny.

This is Canada: the flashpoints of friction often appear between Quebec and the rest of the country, between the old nation-state with its fixed borderlines and the new open state process, between the aboriginals' spiritual rootedness in the land and their trust in dialogue and the settlers' materialism and their demand for permanent resolution, between desires for independence and originality and the need for channels between solitaries, between evolutionary Canada and the revolutionary American empire. What do I mean by evolutionary? A culture and civilization in perpetual, mostly peaceful metamorphosis. What do I mean by revolutionary? A society defined and convulsed by revolution, insurrection, coup or civil war, conditioned by the will to violence, by bruised moods.

A digression: the evolutionary model of Canada especially contrasts with the revolutionary model of America in the notion of solitude. In Canada it is still possible to be alone: in America, there is a relentlessly public existence—the solidarity of the commercial—for everyone, with little quiet left for anyone.

Quebec and Canada need each other because Quebec provides flashes of challenge, a current of passion, while Canada provides fields, a larger frame for that passion. One without the other would enfeeble the whole, leaving in pieces the traces of the grander latent scheme, the light state, fixed and yet unfixed, a new kind of collage country, made of aboriginal dream songs and fierce polemics, private vision and media publicity, the first country to eminently absorb the swing and shock that accompanies the electric infusion, the processing of fire.

———————

Ancient philosophers were familiar with the elemental grounds of their times and places: earth, air, fire and water. Fire, or electrical energy, is our element.

The ancients were also familiar with the method of poetic wisdom. Proofs lead to theory. My method is to make what I write an echo of everything I probe and read, and observe and absorb. A mosaic country needs a mosaic response. What I propose is not a theory, but a story about Canada that is also a poem, an unfinished fragment, a song and a broadside on the country that people elsewhere often overlook.

———————

To arrive at a conclusion is to arrive at a beginning: we will find that debate about who we are is what we are.

I'm drawn to my country's paradoxes and promises—its incompleteness and anomalies, the inward verve and subtle pulse of the magnetic north. Here discontinuities and abiding frictions are necessary for our growth. Here I find a puzzle of great beauty: Canada works well in practice, but just doesn't work out in theory.

We falter forward on obscure, diverging paths: we struggle to make guesses: we come to questions of ruling and state: we envision a place where what is humane has not yet disappeared: we continue to search because we sense that a high form of civilization, of civility, is at stake. "Hurry slowly," the adage says shrewdly. So it must be with us, now.

First Meditation

IN A COMMUNICATION STATE

. . . During his first Canadian winter, [Alexander Graham] Bell had resumed some of his former experiments with tuning forks . . . The harmonic, or multiple, telegraph [prototype of the telephone] was beginning to take shape. He spent hours in the little drawing room . . . singing a single note into the piano, his foot on the pedal, "listening for the answering vibration of corresponding key."

— AVITAL RONELL, describing Bell's thought processes, in *The Telephone Book: Technology, Schizophrenia, Electric Speech*

I perceive communication to be the value of Canada, the highest good of a state where understanding and misunderstanding, conciliatory conversation and vitriol, where constant negotiation and the expansions and limits of language, coexist. We have had to learn how to contact one another over an enormous land space, across five-and-a-half time zones, in what was once a wilderness of scattered settlements, in what is now a sprawl of suburban edge cities and satellite towns. Technology forges connections and disconnections here.

Through the committees and meetings that first established the Canadian map in 1867, through the language controversies and crises of unity, the public debates and referenda that have characterized Confederation, we can pick up, and discern, this story developing: dynamic communication. The story carries a myriad of messages about the necessity of reaching one another, of patiently listening to each other, the urgency of continuous debate, the subtle and ironic recognition that our audacious and original meaning must emerge from conferences, words, communiqués, images, signals, symbols and vibrations sent over the air.

From the beginning Canadians have had to lay track, build roads and bridges, dig canals, string wires from telegraph poles, set up communications networks and centres and transmitters and receivers, establish the complex coordinates of links that will bind one coast to the other, make translations that conduct meaning from one language group to another, in an inextricable dialogue where resolution often seems remote, and unlikely. I take the CN Tower in Toronto to be the power point symbolic of invisible influx and transmission. Its motto: Welcome, Let Your Spirits Soar.

The reverse side of the hunger and need to communicate is the discharge of random chatter. This is the noise that can block out our better instincts, blank out the flow of ethical considerations: the noise can be the grumbling and innuendo, the accusing and blaming, that retreats back into itself, into the political solipsism that we sometimes call regionalism. The communication pattern makes our state a place and condition of multiple voices, not one voice, a polyphony that can become a deafening and stifling cacophony.

This restless communication field makes Canada perpetually difficult to define. Our myth, or cultural mood, differs profoundly from that of the United States, with its individualistic story, its militarism and commercialism, its violent conquests of space and people, its millenarian sense of Manifest Destiny. Creativity and cruelty collide with unparalleled intensity and seductiveness in America. In Canada people hug the borderlines between the provinces and the states, seek associations in cities and towns, construct vital links and support structures (railways, dams, hydroelectric projects, satellites), and then experience the inability to agree on what the country is about. We have formed a consensus to not allow ourselves to be defined by a single unifying idea. Constitutional conferences and advisory committees embody processes of breakdown and gradual rebuilding. Yet many cultures and many often contradictory meanings mingle freely here. Vehement disagreements may mask or obscure the underlying faith that the process of confused and even angry engagement, of stumbling incomprehension, those divisive showdowns that apparently sever goodwill from our experiences, may be the path that leads to the sense of difference and respectful distance that, in another paradox, can reveal the harmony in our humanness.

We resist any final articulation of ourselves and our country because we know, deep in our souls, that our story unfolds the process and value of communication itself. In this wide, spacious country with its areas of privacy and repose, solitude and reverie can lift us and inspire us: here we may think, observe, comment, reflect, interpret and release ourselves from traditional forms so that we may dream. Electronic intensities will deluge us, and they can be channelled: to communicate with others, with our own imaginations and minds, with the landscape and cityscape, through our machines, is our chief business: culture and the possibility of affinity and rapport, our primary hope: and talking and arguing, not to merely fill the time, but an extension of humane interplay beyond our provinces. We know that we have begun without a fixed idea of who we are and of where we are going. The tracks of communication, always shifting, are everything.

The myth of Canada, its hidden story, is of a contemplative country, a place of inwardness, where people can question the idea of nationhood and ponder what values we wish to see expressed and achieved, and what solitudes of identity and reverie we wish to preserve. We wait, in a rendezvous of societies and people, and in this waiting we are often perplexed, tempted by swirls of anger and vengeful hatreds, yet drawn to the energies of the barely spoken, and to traces in the northern air, to the lingering but not entirely comprehended memories of what it took to make this ours, the liberties of a new world.

Remember:

The Confederation debates of 1864–1867.

Representatives from Canada West, or Ontario, from Canada East, or Quebec, and from the Maritimes, gathered in Charlottetown, Quebec City and what was soon to be renamed Ottawa. They met and talked: and talked on, through the long days, into the evenings.

Earnest disputes and speechifying, arguments and caucuses, bargaining and haggling, compromises and trade-offs, grumbling and muttering . . . It was all "coaxing and wheedling," according to George Brown. The process was tentative: it was uncertain, slow, requiring a devotion of hours, and reserves of patience. But the representatives negotiated to make a new transcontinental union. Sir John A. Macdonald affirmed that "This is the second time that man has founded a democracy in the new land . . ."

October 1864, Quebec City.

By day there were meetings, conference room dealings, more words, more accommodations. At night there were dinners, balls, informal conversations, dances and more dances.

Edward Whelan, delegate from Prince Edward Island, said, "The Cabinet Ministers—the leading ones especially—

are the most inveterate dancers I have ever seen; they do not seem to miss a dance the live-long night."

And south of the border?

By September 1864, the American Civil War had reached an agonizing apogee of bloody mania. The Union general Sherman had invaded Atlanta. In October, Confederate general Hood ambushed Sherman outside the burning city—though Hood's assault failed to stall Sherman's advance: at the same time, another Union general, Sheridan, devastated the Shenandoah countryside. By November, Hood had retreated in a shambles, and Sherman had razed Atlanta. Yankees swarmed to the sea, hunting down rebels, destroying railways, looting mansions and farms, torching crops, pillaging food-stores, confiscating farm animals, until the South was humbled in 1865.

To the north, West Canadians, East Canadians and Maritimers argued over unity. When they weren't debating the nature and structure of the new nation, they were stating strong—but not necessarily final—opinions over who should shoulder the better part of the national debt burden.

Remember:

The Canadian experiment was in part inspired by fear of the American Civil War and of the Fenian border raids of the mid-1860s. Aware of the carnage to the south, alarmed by the efficient and restless military power of the victorious Union, Canadian politicians met to talk—and talk—about, and thus conceive through words, a different kind of state.

No one was coerced into signing the British North America Act. During the debates no individual or group was bullied or viciously co-opted, or hustled along by the barrel of a gun, or pricked on the sharp edge of a bayonet. The words that the Fathers of Confederation set down did not dismay or incense any participating members from the three highly disparate regions. English and Québécois politicians alike agreed out of self-interest and a strong sense of self-protective vulnerability to make a state. The Québécois delegation—George-Étienne Cartier was one of its eloquent leaders—was promised that Quebec would have its own system within the larger system, a deliberate and welcomed gesture that preserved a measure of vital dissent inside the new country.

A symbolic or esoteric reading of the negotiations and situations would reveal how Americans battled their fellow

Americans for their new steeled unity, offering their lives in patriotic sacrifice, and that Canadians fought each other over the conference tables, offering arguments, hesitations, compromises and principles for future debate. It appears that when Americans go mad and murderous, Canadians take notes and squabble.

Typically, the unity that the Canadians discovered was loose, provisional, varied and improvised. There was no sense in which a specific identity was being forged: no words were spoken about eternal verities. The document they produced—the British North America Act—was less definite, and entirely less ringing, than the American Declaration of Independence, or, for that matter, the French Declaration of the Rights of Man. The Canadian endeavour must have seemed vague and quixotic, certainly full of paradoxes, in its yoking together of unlikely people, the French and the English, and those who settled the coasts and the interiors. Of course, many people were left out of the arrangement. We see, nevertheless, that *E Pluribus Unum* was achieved with war drums, troop parades and marches, flags, and the shouts of a certain and virtuous cause, marshalled over rubble and corpses. "Peace, Order and Good Government" was achieved through mediation, speechifying and written agreements, and the acknowledgement and guarantee of differences: a process that most understood would have to be long and civil.

Dominion Day, July 1, 1867.

The founding Fathers added "Dominion" at the last moment to the new country's title. What, exactly, did it mean? Their first choice had been "kingdom," which they rejected because of its ominous suggestion of empire. They huddled and mused: then they vetoed "republic" and "confederacy." Many representatives to the conferences stated that "dominion" was obscure, if not arcane, in its meaning. It was soon agreed that the word was mostly ornamental—almost a flourish—an extemporized name to be changed later. "It was rather absurd," sniffed the Earl of Derby, an adviser to the British prime minister, Benjamin Disraeli.

The British ruling class and politicians weren't much interested in Canada, and whether its official title was to be "The Dominion of . . ." or otherwise Disraeli was preoccupied with domestic issues, particularly the Reform Bill that extended voting privileges to a larger British public; he was also distracted by Gladstone's ascension to the leadership of the strengthening Liberals. Political survival dominated Disraeli's mind.

And Queen Victoria's opinion of the word "Dominion"?

"Not a very happy addition," she snorted dismissively.

On the first Dominion Day, people spontaneously erected signs of celebration. Government fiat wasn't necessary. Across the regions there were fireworks and outdoor concerts, and welcoming orations and unfurled banners. Some of the signs conveyed a provocative, even a subversive, discontinuity in their messages: the appearance, once more, of a lack of an overriding ideal or a concept of one prevailing community.

In Nova Scotia people put back a word that had been vetoed by the founding fathers

SUCCESS TO THE CONFEDERACY

And then there was this banner in Quebec

BIENVENUE A LA NOUVELLE PUISSANCE

These signs were loaded with meanings. Overtones, layers. A confederacy means those who league together in a proud covenant but preserve their individuality: in short, a federation. It wouldn't have been lost on the international observers in 1867 that, a short time after the American Civil War and less than a hundred years after the War of Independence, this word heralds, and confirms, rebels and rebellion, and not a revolution.

"*Puissance*" links to the English "puissant," meaning powerful. Its etymology bridges, through the Italian "*possente*," to "potent." The echoes in the word "potent" are significant:

we hear, reverberating, "possible" and "potential." The signs seemed to be summoning welcome to the possibility of the new.

Thursday, March 9, 1876.

The Exeter Place Laboratory, Boston, Massachusetts.

Alexander Graham Bell, resident of Brantford, Ontario, and Thomas Watson, Bell's collaborator and a native of Salem, Massachusetts, worked together to discover a method for transmitting the human voice through the air. They studied sound waves, wires, membranes, tubing, the strange static and oscillations of the unpredictable current and its enigmatic effects. Bell and Watson dipped needles into water inside black boxes. They hoped that reed receivers would relay their voices, carry their conversations.

Their experiments failed, but they persisted.

"I could hear a confused muttering sound like speech," Bell jotted down in his ruminative notebook, "but I could not make out the sense."

Bell's lifelong obsession was hearing. His wife, Mabel, was deaf. His father, Melville, had pioneered a system for teaching the deaf. Called Visible Speech, Melville Bell's system is still in use today. Alexander Bell spent the major part of his life in postures of listening. He paid close attention to what was said and left unsaid—the rhythm of words, the arcane associative echoes and patterns of words and sentences, the gaps between words, and silence. Thomas Watson wrote in his memoirs that he was a mystic, a medium who longed to channel communications from the other side of material existence, who craved access to the invisible. He described how he sought out occult meanings in seances, and participated in white-magic rituals. It hadn't escaped him that he'd been raised in Salem, the site of the notorious witch trials. He felt the passion to listen too.

Listening was both an active and a wise passive state for them. The world was vibrating sound: things were alive with voicings and pulsings. Even to say they looked for a technology that would carry the voice is inaccurate: they explored through the ear, sounding, keening. They were tuning in to what Marshall McLuhan would come to call "acoustic space." Listening also meant for Bell and Watson picking up the subtleties of overtones, the brushings of almost inaudible vibrations. They made themselves receptive to the voices and din that issued from the other side of our supposedly settled dimension. One scientist worked to restore a lost sense to the deaf and to the one he loved: the other yearned to crack channels to the netherworld.

Friday, March 10, 1876.

Bell and Watson tested a brass pipe, a platinum needle and a box with a speaking-tube mouthpiece. The two men then went to separate rooms. They closed the doors between them. Their ensuing exchange is legendary.

The story says that these were the first words uttered over the makeshift line

"Mr. Watson, come here. I want to see you."

Other accounts differ. Bell and Watson, naturally, contradict one another in their notes and records—their inevitable retellings. After the moment of discovery, the first vocal communication through an electrical current, the two scientists couldn't finally agree on what they actually said.

Variations say

"Come here, Watson, I need you."

"Mr. Watson, come here, I want you."

Watson, charged with excitement, scurried into the room where his collaborator sat. It was his turn to speak, and to express his delight. Legend, however, has not chosen to precisely preserve his reply on the line. But it is essential to try to recall a semblance of what might have been said.

"Mr. Bell, do you understand what I say? Do-you-un-der-stand-what-I-say?"

Bell had heard, and had understood. The telephone was born.

The two had indirectly discovered this: no walls or closed doors, and thus no barrier or barricades, can arrest the electric flux, those vital lines, the sometimes seismic circuits of energy, once we have tapped into them. The energy fields will tear away boundary lines, and build and build into greater surges. People may try to manage and influence, and try to channel and even buffer, the urges and leaps and fluctuations and ripples: but no one will be able to stop the metamorphic flow.

A cry for help: a call for connection, and consultation. These calls speak of a need for reaching across abysses to contact one another. There was a crying out with a hope that some assistance would come.

Bell supposedly spilled acid on himself. Then, squirming in pain and shock, he called out for his assistant to come to him. This story is probably apocryphal, the result of Watson's imaginative re-creation through his memoirs. It is the version that schoolchildren are taught, and it is the version that we hear through anecdote, and that we see in movies and TV documentaries.

My point is this: the first words heard over the airwaves were a call for assistance. The Canadian inventor spoke to his American colleague. Both then became confused about what was said.

"Do-you-un-der-stand-what-I-say?"

Help and comprehension: a voice asking for attention: a voice asking for confirmation that a communiqué had been received: a moment of miscommunication: a story retold, re-arranged. People calling to each other; voices asking a question, making the attempt to bridge abysses, to bring news, and even solace.

Bell and Watson knew that the telephone would henceforth always operate on the principle of sympathetic vibrations.

And in the reverberations of their invention breakthrough, the electric wires buzzed with a vulnerable message, an urgent tone and ambiguous words, with the pitch of vital minds engaged in the insistent urge to discover meaning, the track of emotion, the search to find a sympathetic pulse and echo in other people, and the world, the necessity of response.

Signal Hill, Newfoundland, December 12, 1901.

Guglielmo Marconi was flying a kite in a storm. After his receiving towers had been smashed down by the wind, he'd improvised by attaching an antenna to the kite and letting it soar up into the rain and clouds. Marconi was determined to prove that over-the-horizon reception was possible, that radio waves would follow the curvature of the earth and so defy Euclidean law.

His kite endured the storm's blast. He'd arranged with his colleagues in England to have a wireless message sent across the ocean. Shortly after 12:30 p.m., his associates in Cornwall telegraphed this cryptic code.

A single letter filtered through the squall.

"S . . ."

Three clicks: in Morse code.

Marconi listened on an earphone to the pulses that leapt from over 3,300 kilometres away. He'd become the first person to hear the other side of the world through technology. His experiment proved that radio waves would travel long-distance without wires. Unseen power lines could criss-cross the globe, the energies they carried looking for receivers, for interpreters.

This intercontinental message was limited to what appeared to be a fragment: S. Out of fragments come implications. Symbolists would say that S stands for the snake of energy, the serpentine cosmos, twisting, uncoiling in strings vibrating, life itself in its capacity to endlessly recharge and endure: a symbol, then, of renewal. In the mystic reading of the world, the letter S is identified with lunar influences and tides, and with the harmony of opposites.

Turn the S on its side, complete the figure to make it resemble the figure eight, and you will recognize the symbol for infinity. S also symbolizes waves, their undulating form, their transient shape. It is the letter that evokes the constant subatomic hiss of electromagnetism, the persistent sound of nature's energy, once again both waves and fields.

Newfoundland did not join Confederation until 1949. Nevertheless, Signal Hill in St. John's has entered the mythology of a country obsessed with methods of communication linkage. On Signal Hill, an Italian inventor demonstrated that wireless messages would zigzag over the sea, extending ourselves into the atmosphere, allowing access to other languages, symbols, places, voices, sounds, filling the air with more of the human tone.

And air is the element of lightness.

Canadians quickly embraced radio technology. Across the country, teenagers built their own crystal sets, and discovered that the night was the best time for reception. Darkness always intensifies hearing, and touch. They were sometimes probing the dark with copper-wire feelers, listening to distant tinny voices. In 1920 the radio presence in Canada was confirmed by the first world broadcast of live music by CFCX in Montreal. Their programming consisted entirely of music—and weather reports.

Here is the pattern:

One communication story outlines the shape of civility—of tact and trust—of a recognition of the other (of difference, of necessary and enduring strangeness), and of an unusual partnership formed in a loose, mostly peaceable confederation. This is the storyline that emerges when we look deeply at how the Fathers of Confederation gathered and welcomed debate on nation-building. It is the process that stressed the lack of definition, the improvisational nature, of the agreement they called, with careful (and masterful) understatement, the BNA Act.

The other stories outline a hidden but latent narrative: how we have tapped into energy sources and resources, spheres of radiating influence, emanating powers that allowed and inspired the invention and proliferation of communications technologies. We see experimenters working to discover ways of reaching others, bridging space, compressing time, allowing the miraculous cosmos to speak through us, pulling from the air a live tradition, energies moving. Through the confusions and misapprehensions, the re-creations and the often mixed motives of the experimenters came higher ways of communicating, of enlarging how much we can each actually say or deliver to one another.

———————

Encounters and valedictions, summons and replies. Questions and requests, probing and pulses. The communication of meaning, the desire to cross those abysses that lie between us, in space, and in our minds, implies an act of heart—a receptivity that could lead to embarrassment and pain, to muddle and contention. But that desire to communicate—to reach out—is also a gesture of trust. We become hosts for the guests of speech. This is the trust that an essential code will be passed on between discrete people, between the cosmos and ourselves.

Discovery, experimentation, confusion, error, the tensions of wildfire liberty and the rage or need for order—these factors are part of what has been evolving, in a way sometimes obscure to our own eyes. The communications stories show developing technologies and memoranda, and their gradual convergence into the data-rush we have come to witness, and facilitate, and document, and admit. And they reveal the longing for connection, to be participants in creation through relaying and interpreting that rush.

Sir Wilfrid Laurier said, in an often quoted statement, "The twentieth century belongs to Canada." Again these words are layered with ambiguities, meanings Laurier himself no doubt didn't intend or foresee. The word "belongs" links to the medieval English *langien*, which means to crave for, to long after. Laurier's proclamation suggests a golden future awaits the Canadian experiment. His phrase does not suggest the expansions of empire. It hints that Canada could provide a civilized foundation on which modernity can work out a destiny that differs from other fresh-born cultures.

I've juxtaposed the Fathers of Confederation with Wilfrid Laurier with Alexander Graham Bell, Thomas Watson and Guglielmo Marconi to show how Canada is an experiment in an alternative current. I call it a communication state: this is the condition of receptivity, the pattern of listening and probing, and dialogue and misunderstanding, of broken messages and missed connections, of perpetual mediation and trial through technology, of reading the signs and scanning for signals.

The only way we can live in this country is through advanced technologies of communication. We need the telephone, the telegraph, the radio, the satellite dish, TV and computer screens, air travel and trains. The paradox is these technologies do not solidify individual identity: they do not focus a singular identity for anyone. Electricity scatters individual being, conjuring ghostly simulations. It transmits shards of apparently disconnected data, pieces in a riddle that is a part of a greater enigma. Tribes, clubs, corporations and cults can arise from the powerful discharge from TV sets, radios, telephones, computer networks: the isolated individual may find that isolation all the more acute when there is such a tumble of seemingly incoherent information, with the result that it becomes easier to hand power over to a larger group, someone to make decisions for you. Yet electronic technologies spur and excite more questions, allow for multiple points of view—never have there been such a multitude of people speaking, appearing, on our screens, through our speakers—and add to the strange sensation of fusion with world events, coupled with an often distraught confusion over the significance and intent of those events. Communication technologies can appear to have a life of their own, immersing us, threatening us: they sometimes seem to be capable of dehumanizing and dislocating our lives, and of enhancing our awareness, sending out images and reflections of ourselves everywhere, anywhere, anything at anytime.

In this global electric city, we are haunted by a sense of presence, the trace of something close, almost there. Is that presence supernatural, immanent, or is it our human world amplified, echoing, calling, yearning, crying out? Could it be both? The electroscope is a realm of emanations and radiance, music and mystery.

Debate and energy's flow, a country established over a bargaining table, a myth made out of vibrations in the air . . .

Canada has a hermetic past: its meanings are concealed in private utterances, in whisperings among interrupted signals, in insoluble arguments that are meant to promote further arguments about unity, in misread messages and in quiet resistance to the pressure to join into one supreme monolithic political system. I suggest that Canada has a discontinuous, contradictory character. Without a singular purpose or pre-determined historic goal—no violent imposition or expression of a homogenous political ideology or myth—Canadians have lived with, and have invited, many stories, moods and visions that must come with many different kinds of people and voices.

Patterns only become clear in retrospect. When we ponder and interpret, then different levels of readings will reveal themselves. The Canadian patterns often look misty or un-defined to visitors and to our own commentators who wish to have clear resolution to every angle, so we stoop to define ourselves through what we are not (neither American nor British nor French). The communications stories hint that the Canadian artifact has always been a through-zone, adapt-able and reflective, a medium through which the questions, calls, pulses and ideas may pass.

The historian Arthur Lower is said to have commented that Canada's strength is her anonymity. This is a well-known and often reworked remark. Like many Canadian figures, A.R.M. Lower led a double life: he wrote humorous squibs under the pseudonym L.E.G. Upper. The comment attributed to Lower has endured. People often say we are faceless, blending in easily, disappearing into familiar and even unfamiliar environments. When people stereotype others into distinct national personae—the gregarious American, the aloof French, the condescending British, the brooding Russian—they speak of the quiet Canadian, the unassuming voyager in the world's political systems and cultures.

I'll adapt Lower's remark and call the anonymity part of our invisibility, our chameleon nature. Quietness outside, turbulence within. We have in Canada acknowledged three founding peoples—French, English and Aboriginal: we have encoded three official languages, French and English of course, and the right of the Aboriginal people to speak their native tongue in the legislature of the territory Nunavut. Yet writers and commentators over the years have declared that few can say what a Canadian is. It is as if our identities are kept hidden, like diary entries that no one is meant to read and whose meaning is clear only to their author.

We recognize secret sides to ourselves. Our most mythologized prime ministers—Wilfrid Laurier, Mackenzie King, John Diefenbaker, Pierre Trudeau—exude fascination in part because their characters, motives, dreams and actions often remain complex, unfathomable. When literary critics referred to the one true Canadian theme of survival and victimhood—an outgrowth of the ideology of cultural nationalism in the 1960s—we were apt to nod our heads and mutter mildly, "Well, maybe . . . if you insist." The sixties' nationalists concerned themselves with clear definitions and definitive answers. But we continue to glimpse through guesses, hunches, rumours, traces, intimations that our deepest resource is in flux and inward destinies, what is quixotic, tentative, sometimes withdrawn, exploratory, a process that refuses finished explanations and a fixed point of arrival.

It may be that we know how the anonymous Canadian, who lives in a place where communications links are a matter of air and vibrations and hints and crossed wires, has no need for a static identity. It may be that this counter-nation, our eclectic mosaic culture, this condition of being seemingly disparate and separate (exceptional societies within the whole society; regional tensions; the city-state that is now Toronto; Aboriginal land claims), all our obsessions with who we are, is our strength, our promising path, our myth, our original form of harmony.

Multiple, mobile perspective is vital for perceiving the effects of the global electric city. In the electronic culture of speeding and disruptive bits of information, ideological or fundamentalist rigidity, dialectical imperatives and dogmatic authority may help to make reality temporarily clear, but the truth of our experience is variety, paradox, concealed destinies, interconnection, latent forms, strange uncertainties, signatures of people and aeons that we are still learning how to read. Lewis Thomas writes about the data deluge in *The Lives of a Cell*, evoking the streaming of images and words

> Somewhere, obscured by the snatches of conversation, pages of old letters, bits of books and magazines, memories of old movies, and the disorder of radio and television, there ought to be more intelligible signals. Or perhaps we are only at the beginning of learning how to use the system, with almost all of our evolution . . . still ahead of us . . .

Canadians, I've said, are capable of wearing masks, capable of flexible positions and improvised responses, acknowledgements of the provisional and the variant. Some say this is bland: others call it civility, and tact, a high order of polite and camouflaged civilization. I say that these are an insight into what it means to exist in a planetary culture, where private identity must be cloaked if it's to maintain solitude, and thus make time for the cultivation of the inner person.

———————

Esoteric writings speak of veiled destinies of eminence—the promise of unfolding being—in cryptic codes, styles often difficult for modern people, accustomed to the quick fixes of formulaic clarities and judgments. Who are we? What can we be? The alchemists said we are each amorphous, disorganized, a mystifying set of divisions and contradictions: conventions imposed on us by our societies appear to set our limits of being: we become what others say we are. Each person is a microcosm of heaven and hell, of angelic and demonic conflicts. So the hermetic philosophers asked their pupils to find the still-point of meaning inside, the point of self-transcendence, the web centre of being from which we always depart, to which we can return. Esoteric language is richly imaginative and metaphoric: it expresses the essential desire for individual transformation. Elusive intent, the mining for gold, spirit, introspection: we search to know what is best and worst in us, what can be transmuted into truths that yield disciplines of possibility.

The audacious communication philosophies that developed in Canada, the thinking of Harold Innis, George Grant and Marshall McLuhan, pointed to the unfixed quality in the Canadian soul. Innis and Grant, drenched in tragic readings of history, reacted with foreboding and sorrow in their books. A country so vulnerable and anonymous could easily lose its bearings, and become prey to the monopolies and hunger of the American empire. Grant wrote, "No small country can depend for its existence on the loyalty of its capitalists." McLuhan responded with his customary ambivalence and satiric defiance (he once quipped that he remained in Canada because it gave him unending sources of annoyance, and therefore he was always kept awake)—saying that our un-formed condition could be an informed one. It could be a contemplative position that could become both observant and infused with potential.

Questions linger: what will be the patterns that allow Canadians to move into the future? We missed the vicious civil wars and liberating revolutions of nineteenth- and early-twentieth century nationalism. Is our loose federation a para-digm for the electric city of the teleworld? What could be the result of our unusual symbiosis of technology and raw human need? Somewhere in the information boom we may have lost a wisdom that could be reclaimed. Canada may be fast-forwarding, jump-starting, into a new pattern, a model of communication linkages, a civilization that is more than a grab for power and dominance, a place that could channel the fires of the global wirings, where political alliances are subject to electrical ebb and flow, and the alchemical cultivations of imagination and perception, of the self, could prevail over the ideology of capital.

I'll close my first meditation with thoughts on noise and data.

There are several possible etymologies for the word "noise." One stresses the old French, the Provençal origins, "*nauza*," "*noisa*," "*neuiza*." "Nausea" and "nauseous" stem from these roots. "Noisome" comes from them too. The latter is an archaic word that means troubling, or irritating. Obviously, noise is something that can make you sick. I've found another reading, another echo. "Noise" may come from "*nous*," the Greek word for "mind." From the same Greek root we get "mood," "mode," "atmosphere," the tone of a time and place. Teilhard de Chardin's word, "noosphere," evoking the developing ring of consciousness around the world, mind embodied in the vibrations of circling communications, also has its root in "*nous*." Noise, then, is the roar of the age, voices on the verge of being heard, rhythms not yet fully registered, the shape of things to come. News—another word linked to "*nous*"?—always follows and rises in the din. Yet the new appears slightly out of the reach of our immediate grasp and response.

Different noises reverberate in the air. One is media junk— the strains of data, the clamour of too many reports, slogans, bulletins, opinions, experts' advice, consultants' templates, diagnoses, prognoses, accounts. Mystics speak of this tumult when they describe the soul's chatter that can block out spiritual practice and learning, which lead to concentration, and the hope and aim of an inner coherence of self.

Noise can also become a siren's call, a warning, a yelp, a howl for help, the junk suddenly turning into an expression of people's suffering and need. Call this the new, the chaos of new voices stirring. These are the mutterings and low-frequency pulses of the language we don't yet know, the evolving articulation of myths and symbols, of independent providences, the universes each soul re-creates. When world models collide, stories of reality overlap.

Media noise is the result of an excess of TV, radio broadcasts, computer printouts, polls, Muzak, headlines, statistics and graphs. Mania of too much information, the mercilessness of disjointed input. A diffusion and oppression of your senses and ideas occur when the images and bytes don't connect or cohere. Communications then become garbled, and human voices may be overwhelmed.

Inside the same data-mass, there may appear another set of messages. This is polyphony, the plurality of different approaches, a syncretic communion of interpretations. Pluralism is not relativity. In this polyphony, every individual has one voice with which to speak, two ears with which to listen. Each voice carries a portion of value, no matter how unpalatable or distasteful that voice may be: no one person, government, ideology, transnational, or religious institution can own and dominate the whole.

In our global culture, the chatter and input can tranquilize us, numb us, shear or warp our perceptions. Simultaneously, the blare and pressure is the chaos out of which other structures of consciousness will emerge.

We live in a time of noisy nights and days. Like the nation-builders who sat down to talk, we have the opportunity to peacefully debate and argue. Like Bell listening for his colleague, and like Watson listening for Bell, each of them doing so through closed doors and walls, over makeshift wiring, we search for sympathetic vibrations, and what it means to listen to one another. Like Marconi with his improvised antenna, we work to receive messages, and to recognize the codes and patterns, and to supply and affirm human tones.

I said that I perceived communication to be the value of Canada. This myth could move in a myriad of directions. One story accelerates towards an economic-political crash, bafflement and frustration, disappointment in political leaders of whatever affiliation, a shutdown of faith in the future, and people retreating behind the walls of ethnic and racial loathing and rivalries. Another story reveals the need for people to find ways of bridging abysses. We share in the memory of the call for help over the airwaves; the vulnerability of the admission, that confession. And we've forgotten the story of the nation-builders who went on talking, despite their fears and skepticism—their resentments and disagreements—and who knew that Canada's spirit must be a poly-valent, accommodating one.

Electronic technologies will sweep us into shocking patterns and unexpected relations. Every element in all the communications stories suggests that in this process of crack-up and discovery, the electric initiation, Canada's lack of definition—its lightness—is its strength.

In the roar of their media-saturated environments, our politicians and leaders become deaf to the noise of the people they represent. These are the voices carrying the clues and cues that telegraph

Do—not—let—
our—experiment—
slip—
from us—

Interlude

ON JUSTICE

Questions keep coming, and coming, over the air, onto our screens, through to us, into our minds and our daily concerns, more all the time. We sense how the wiring of the teleworld ignites and buzzes with crackling intensities and outcries, in an endless recharging of itself. Electrodynamism is not a thing, an object, but an enlarging, and enduring, process of actions and reactions. Thus we are being filled with errant vibrations, feeling the effects of energies passing over into us and from us, receiving that supernatural sensation of an unlimited communication now taking place.

———————

Massive forces drive the technological borderless order. But a primary force, in these seedling moments where so much grows and spreads, appears to be production: the market, fuelled by fierce desire. Electrical fire and the fire of greed kindle economics. In that flux, nations become digitized commodities on stock-exchange floors and on investors' rating screens. A country becomes a product to be rated for its obedience to paying off deficits and debts.

————————

What is justice in this race? How do you pose ethical, spiritual considerations—the consideration of human value, not financial value—in the revved jolts of nomadic economies?

————————

John Stuart Mill said justice is doing as little harm as possible. (I've often wondered if the emphasis in Mill's definition should be on the words "doing . . . little.") Justice is also living harmony—the marriage of opposites. But we engage and are engulfed by organizations that put economics, and even war, first, displacing issues of the good, and of justice itself.

These are what I take to be the four keys to civilized life, a humane existence: liberty, recognition of self-worth (by which I mean education and worthy employment should be available to all), universal health care, equality of opportunity. These four keys honour the person. Any political-economic system, whether governed by parties of the left or of the right, which seeks to degrade or diminish the worth of a person, can't be a spirit moving towards the fulfillments of a good life.

————————

But when technology finally penetrates or permeates all spheres of life, we have reason to fear that uniformity will be the result. If the telephone was invented and constructed on the principle of sympathetic vibrations, then the dance of electricity guarantees that there will be a shadow effect that will accompany the invention—an effect that will show itself in an unsympathetic repercussion, restrictions placed on empathy and conscience, a narrowing down of perspective, a slamming shut of the doors of perception. To maintain the harmonies of contradictions, both vibrations need to be apparent to us: if it is only the shadow that appears, we become blinded—or routed in a direction that could be self-annihilating.

We feel more, know more, in the electrodynamism of the planetary culture, often whether we wish to or not. To protect what may be the deep rule of living—the harmony of conflicts—we must pose probing against numbness, a courageous gentleness against ferocity and cruelty, justice against growing inequities and terror, humility and receptivity against fantasies of omnipotence, the prizing of the soul against exploitation.

There must be engagement: there must be protest.

Letter to Those in Power

If the leaders of mankind were more aware, when by chance they come into minor powers they might exploit others less.

—From *The Gateless Gate*,
a collection of koans first recorded
by a Chinese Zen master in A.D. 1228

To the rulers
To those who exercise the power to command

How do I address a state of mind? How do I speak to, and challenge, what is becoming the global paradigm—a dogmatic thought pattern that slashes across political alliances, a force of mind so pervasive that few know how to oppose it? Who is there to answer for the desensitizing, the "adapt or perish" economic survivalism, the disconnected abstractions that elevate matter into a first and only principle, the apotheosis of technology so that it becomes the answer rather than a part of the human question and quest, the equation of markets and production with democracy and liberty that we encounter in almost every system? If the transnational corporations are the decisive players of the planetary culture, then who specifically do you address?

The corporatist-economic model of society appears to be governing us. Economists, often in the pay of transnationals, are deciding, for us, what democracy is, and will be. There have been political advocates of the economy-first state of mind—Brian Mulroney in Canada, George Bush Sr. and

Newt Gingrich in the United States, Margaret Thatcher in England—but they are shells, speakers on behalf of the politics of the bottom line who do not always appear to directly embody the forces shaping, rearranging our choices. To be incorporated means to belong to one body: to be absorbed, or swallowed. Those snared on the material plane of existence, without receptivity to the pouring down of imaginative and spiritual knowledge, rule us—and the result is the crisis in leadership and governance we witness. We have handed management and influence over to market strategists and the transnationals who can afford the new technology systems. But how do they lead? How do they speak to us? Is theirs the struggle of the soul to encounter and integrate its shadows? Is theirs the struggle between matter and spirit? The market triggers the furies of invention—the powers of production. What has taken hold, however, is the ascendancy of the market without alternatives. Tyranny looms when you can find no way out.

How can we shift the view away from the consensual hallucination called deficit and debt reduction? Those in power have given authority to the corporatist-collective mindset, which is supported by the inflamed organisms of electronic technology.

Here is the reverse angle of the flexible confederation with its communication story: it is a state that can become vulnerable to transnational despotism. We stand at the beginning of what could be the most spiritual and humane century—a light age coming—a renaissance of wonders, culture, science, politics, commerce and communication rejoining: and we experience the terror and ecstasy, the trauma and learning, that erupt in the spiralling confusion. Yet what we call "nationhood" or "sovereignty" no longer appears to describe or evoke our rattled, fluid state.

And this question rises above others: What will it cost to remain Canadian in the fury of global production?

The economic survivalism that possesses most societies elevates the energetic marketing of things to a first principle. But surely we should ask, What is the supposed ecstasy of production for? Who, or what, profits? Is there a compass we can find in the borderless economies, where money free-flows everywhere? If massive trading systems are a necessity—which, apparently, they are—then what will happen to that experiment called Canada, an alternative current, when it is so melded and diffused?

Economics are about states of mind: they express moods. We give the market animal names—bull, bear—give the boom and bust cycles the titles of seasons. The market is subject to tremors and jitters: currency levels react to news like a thermostat of the psyche. Computers web cities and countries into reactive coils: the market dawns, closes: it jumps and dives. It appears to operate on principles that, while begun in the need for liberal originality—in Adam Smith's elevation of ingenious individuals to primary value—now operate through impersonal force, abstract conglomerations: powers that exist beyond most individuals. With production elevated to a holy order, we guarantee the lack of civil guidance, of kindness. Kind: from the source word "kin," or "kindred," meaning affinity and relationship. Kind: it suggests the knowledge that what we do must affect and move the whole person, matter, spirit, mind, soul. The crisis of governing becomes one of affinity, thus of imagination.

In Canada, we have watched our governments, federal and provincial, merge the energies of production with ruling. And in this merger we've observed these assumptions surface and dominate: dismantle the idea of a government responsive to any citizen, drive issues of governing away from questions of inequality, ethics, environmental protection, dehumanization, push the question of citizen engagement away from the broad public sphere into the narrowed zones of homes and neighbourhoods therefore limiting individual influence in the overall system (make citizens in fact feel they will never have much of an influence), promote the language of trade and unfettered production so that people begin to feel uncomfortable when they hear any argument or proposition not deemed "realistic," hand power over to unelected officials in institutions identified only by gnomic abbreviations like the IMF or the WTO, provoke and maintain the fear that we will somehow lose "most favoured nation status" with currency speculators, make force the ultimate act of consumption, cut massively into areas where people need more investment (in education and health, in the arts and in scientific research), change the symbolism of Canada from a place with an enigmatic and shrouded evolutionary spirit to an investment property meant for a fire sale.

Every movement has its manifestos.

I found one in *A New Direction for Canada: An Agenda for Economic Renewal,* presented to the House of Commons by Michael H. Wilson, finance minister in Brian Mulroney's Conservative government, on November 8, 1984. Wilson coloured his paper blue. His manifesto reveals what afflicts us now.

We find in its pages the corporatist *perestroika,* the reinvention of government. (It is astonishing how revolutionaries of whatever political stripe begin with the premise that all government is human, all too human, and so must go. They then seek to replace it with a force that is suprahuman—efficient, clean, precise and above all sleek, like a godly machine that will run on its own.) In Michael Wilson's bland introduction, we nevertheless discover plans, projections, hypotheses, deductions: the call for complete reform. Soulless mind exposes itself here. We see the rule of international bureaucrats.

The first pages signal that the target of the attack will be the debt. Wilson lambastes

"... expansive, intrusive government ..."

". . . a country that had not kept pace with . . .
change . . ."
". . . economic policies which, though often well-
intentioned, have been erratic, have discouraged pro-
ductivity . . ."
". . . regulation and intervention . . ."

He raises "the judgement of those in the marketplace" to the
highest order. Wilson claims nothing less than a complete
"economic reconstruction" will suffice to pull Canada from
the brink of bankruptcy. The implication being, we are a
country that shouldn't exist, given its ineptitude. To whom
does Wilson answer? We can't feel his soul—it's buried under
the bland prose of committee recommendations. Sentences
leak that there are foreign investors, unnamed speculators
who will not pronounce Canada to be a sound commodity
until the government undertakes drastic measures of curtail-
ment—cut and slash. Again, from this proclamation

"Failure to control our deficit when others are con-
trolling theirs would undermine confidence . . ."
". . . new competitive realities in the world marketplace . . ."
". . . government subsidies have distorted market
signals . . ."
". . . government has become too big . . ."

Then I found a passage written before the Free Trade
Debate erupted and threatened to snap the country in two,

long before Prime Minister Mulroney said anything about economic integration with the United States. The Wilson committee plants their land mine

> ". . . if we are to foster growth through trade, we must obtain more secure improved access to foreign markets on the broadest possible basis. This would require, of course, that Canada would also have to move to increase access to its domestic market . . ."

The Wilson corporation goes on to describe "the adjustment that free trade would entail." There will be a lot of talk about this "adjustment."

Give the Wilson committee its due. They ask hard questions, phrasing problems well on the realistic plane of things, thinking like tough-minded banking advisers or ambitious accountants. There are, they insist, "the limits of budgetary realities." They inform us that "some of the changes necessary for an economic turnaround called for strong medicine." This will come to mean the review of government agencies, Via Rail, the CBC, the National Energy Program, Petro-Canada, the Foreign Investment Review Agency, child benefits, Employment Insurance, benefits for the elderly, the so-called Mother Society policies. If the Wilson committee hints at levying a new sales tax, it does so in dim terms, saying that raising revenues "by other means" may be necessary.

Michael Wilson himself read this manifesto in the House of Commons. He undoubtedly delivered it in his monotonous boardroom style, a manner so mandarin and dispassionate, as flat as the realistic plane he wants to occupy, that only the most obsessive observer would stay awake to pay attention. In the corporatist reality the best way to deliver a sensational or controversial message is to do so in the guise of someone who knows better than you do. Let us do the thinking for you; settle down; all is in control; no need to ask questions. If you make things sound inoffensively obvious, then it is likely no one will listen closely.

Recall that Prime Minister Mulroney distanced himself from the corporatist call. He said the blue-paper contained mere recommendations—it was no template or blueprint. Recall that no federal election was held to debate the proposals and precepts of the Wilson committee's formulae. Yet the words—for all their calculated dullness—are proclamations by souls gone cold.

I'll quickly review common denominators in the corporatist mission

   ... the free market is absolutely good ...
   ... government interference is always inept ...
   ... deficits are always the problem ...
   ... we are accountable to international currency speculators, therefore subject to restrictions of time ...
   ... we must compete in the global marketplace by immediately joining a vast North American trade structure ...

Let me add: the corporatist state of mind is epically driven by pressures of structure and time. The shorter the time frame of investment and reward, the greater the intensity of demand: the larger the structure, the more that structure must absorb the person. From the business think-tanks to the institutes of public policy to the committees on trade relations to the business councils we would find these tenets, with slight variations, to be the prevailing ones.

The Wilson committee implied the question: Can we afford Canada? If you agree with the logic of their analyses, then your answer would have to be no: Canada makes no sense whatsoever. If you make linear economics the single vision of your thought, then there is no good reason to pursue an original experiment north of the 49th parallel. We are simply "another trading partner," not truly different.

Things become oddly murky in the blue-paper, however. The committee recites reams of numbers. They push percentages. Graphs chart dips and swells of financial statistics. Long lists of facts mix with mathematical figures. (Who reads this sort of material? And where would you read it? . . . On the subway, hurtling underground? . . . In an airplane, hurtling high over people's homes?) Prophecies predict narratives of boom and bust, supported by arcane diagrams, curiously joyless analyses of the future. The minds that made this seem to have been mesmerized by screens, digital flashing ones and zeros. They conjured graph projections out of figures and ambitious guesswork. Experts and their onscreen flow charts can easily hypnotize anyone eager for an absolute answer to complex questions. You feel those pressures, though, to produce, to use time, to submit to economic structures greater than you, to let capital move where it will.

This manifesto must be the first major political tract ever written in the passive voice. I'm speaking of characterless prose, written as if by no one. There is no "I" or even a "we." Linking verbs abound. There is a mystique of godlike generality and fiat. This depersonalized language tells us that no individual can be held directly responsible for what's said and done. "Employment will do this . . ." "Expenditures reductions will be difficult . . ." "The government attaches top priority . . ." "Concern has been expressed . . ." The document's pages ooze with departmental oil. It blends anything personal with the apparent omniscient force of an omnipotent technological model.

I see a cut-off from emotion in the blueprint. Its prose flattens out and hides the harsh "adjustment." The committee's gospel doesn't reveal how there must be loss, hurt, disarray, perplexity. The carefully developed neutral tone, designed to sound objective, masks how this is only one group of people offering their opinion.

With this use of the passive voice, we see a triumph of the corporatist state of mind over an individual's breath, over tone and imagination, over intuition, attentive language, flexibility, personal voice and distinct cadence: all that would make a tract of writing sound and move like embodied personality, being in the beat of speaking, so that a reader can respond to the breathing of another. In the mathematical abstractions of deficits and GNPs, we see a triumph of structure over personality, individual mystery. During this time of shifting world paradigms—the move from industrial mechanism to electric sensation and digital simulation—we must surely ask for a visionary pragmatism from our politicians and leaders, an engagement that emerges from perpetual questioning, debate about the principles of power, about authority, the complexities of influence and the spending of our considerable wealth.

But the Wilson committee blueprint declared that the enemy of the people is the government. And these were representatives of the government speaking. How ironic, and how suicidal. I challenge the corporatist dogma: in a planetary culture of entwined economies, of people communicating across borderlines through the electronic media, where data hurtles and jams at the speed of light, where we live bathed in TV emanations and radio waves, how can we say that government will always be the enemy of the people? People in government can be brutal, authoritarian: their actions can be monolithic, and stupid. John Locke wrote that a government's mandate is provisional. Its authority exists solely in a contractual, lease-like position with citizens. The protection of rights is the government's sole purpose, Locke said. Jean-Jacques Rousseau wrote that government must always be moved according to the public will—and therefore is contingent on individual engagement. But the corporatists appear to want to replace government with an efficiency model, and obedience to that call has led us to a breakdown of trust in what people of goodwill can do in office.

Leaders often speak of the cynicism and sour-mindedness of citizens. I hear people speak, continually, about the disconnection from human affairs and concerns in those who govern. When I read through the numbers and platitudes of this corporatist manifesto, I recalled how most people in subsequent governments have chosen to shield themselves in statistics, polls, graphs, percentages, that seemingly innocuous terminology of "adjustments." And when I looked closely at the characterless style of the Wilson committee's blueprint, I kept asking: who—and, now, ominously, what—runs the state? And who is it for?

Have we yielded our unfolding story and destiny to the mass organizations that go under the names of GATT and NAFTA? Are we being governed for "the benefit of foreign interests"? Our leaders have helped to unravel the checks on power established by previous regimes, between the state and transnationals and unions, between small businesses and academies and mass media: government has withdrawn—retreated—from its mediation role in society.

(When Canada joined NAFTA, a small economy melded with the most powerful one in the world. There are few similarities between our situation and that of the European Common Market, where old cultures, tested and refined over many generations, exist in strong, though uneasy, partnerships.)

Political and business leaders are responsible for policy and indirectly responsible for the moods and emotions of a place and time. Through legislation, public acts, speeches and gestures, a political leader may affect both a country's economy and its cultural and moral life. The leader's role is about emotion, the general will, so Rousseau said, and about policy. What is the perception many people have of the elected, and of the effects of business and political leadership on our moods? It is one of absence, of automatic actions, of the compulsion to use force, and the uttering of clichés. It is of directions that were not vividly imagined, honestly debated, prepared for, and constantly re-examined. We see the inability of governments to respond to rapid metamorphoses, and so we see rulers who can't hear the scramble and desperation of people who have been callously discarded by the fissions and transfers, the demands and recalibrations of the borderless order. Prolonged recession became a euphemism for depression. We see government setting deficit control and efficient fiscal operation over fairness, equity— creation of conditions where support can be scaled back without loss of opportunity or dignity. The main streets of the planetary culture veer every day into mean streets. Free trade often pushes down wages, promotes protectionist policies—precisely the opposite of what its advocates claimed it would do. (One political observer called NAFTA "a race to the bottom.") And when governments slash into programs in the name of financial reform and tax cuts, they invariably tear into the funding that sustains roads, schools, welfare, the post office, public buildings, museums, art galleries, publishing houses, symphonies, theatres. We have witnessed prime ministers claim that they would strengthen the Canadian federal experiment, and then allowed what has always been an unsettling prospect to come out of the murky atmosphere: complete economic assimilation into the United States.

And yet we have released ourselves to wander the world through electrical connections—light-flyers, light-gliders in our imaginations, and at our keyboards: and we know the cool wind and white wonder of the North. If this is so, then surely a new deal should accompany our evolution. Surely with expanded consciousness—projection into the planetary culture—must come acute responsiveness.

What kind of people rule us? Who are they who purport to lead? Observe our leaders in most political parties, and we often sense something missing in them. Some elected officials and business leaders show admirable traits of toughness: they can bob and weave—they can take a punch, though punch-drunk boxers eventually lose their timing. Some are dogged campaigners, canny tacticians. They may even be sincere.

We should be asking, What sort of inwardness have you cultivated? Where does your soul reach? What air do you breathe? What are you made of, and what do you love? And without a grasp of human suffering, the moral dilemmas and riddles of our existence every day, they can become "denatured." This is the word both Edmund Burke and Samuel Taylor Coleridge used to describe politicians who have no awareness of what effect their actions have on others. We can see the corporatist state of mind, conditioned by financial structures and their compulsions of time, appears to have lost its soul-root in the imagination. What I mean by this is the loss of the ability to sympathize with suffering and confusion, weakness and fear—that awful fear that may stall the movements of spirit and mind—to feel for people and what they do and can't do. The corporatist-committee mind seems incapable of transcending the hypnotism of geometry and categorical solutions, "Single Vision and Newton's sleep," in Blake's words. The imagination: the key to the soul, to seeing pattern in incongruity, to reclaiming the inherent order of the cosmos, to augury and omen, to the realm where we may say we are capable of a destiny and of eminence—a passionate living—to the restoration and contemplation of mystery, to the recognition—sometimes difficult—that there is always a person, another potential seed for consciousness, behind every word, in every place, on every street, in every house or room. The imagination seals us in rainbow covenants with the world. It takes the world—its rawness—back into ourselves, so that we may know more and find more, synchronicities, infinite correspondences, and so we may keep grappling with enigmas. If you press on with more questioning, you may, with courage, find yourself going back eventually to first questions, the graze and edge of what was put to us at the mystical beginning, that asked what is in you, what direction are you travelling, what road are you following, what compass are you using? So in Canada, without a visionary inkling, a breaking through, we will be without strangeness, little more than another greedy place, a seething and frustrating society, perhaps eventually vicious, another armed camp where people grow suspicious or terrified of alien neighbours, another spot on the map to be torn apart by insidious ignorance and myopia, a blip on a TV or computer screen like a distant flashbulb going off in the darkness,

another footnote to the saga of empires, some minor adden-
dum to other histories, other destinies.

TV mercilessly, sometimes ecstatically, exposes us. It is part of what it means to be alive in the wired consciousness that Teilhard de Chardin called the noosphere. Its rays will disclose and exalt the lines, marks, shapes and shadows in a face. The cathode gun behind the screen can brighten and inform appearance, probing and recasting features and expressions, as if the screen was becoming at times more an instrument, uncannily offering something other than spectacle and diversion. The screens, TV or VDT, in occasional brilliant spots, transmit glimpses of our souls, blinding metaphysical instants. What the screens have divulged about the rulers, the powers, is the divorce in them between thought and feeling. The screens have X-rayed rule by necessity and dogmatic will alone. But whose necessity and whose will?

The moving images and sound bites also record and replay, imprint and display, the faces and voices of people who have been bruised, frightened, left distraught and left behind. The screens have caught suffering, etching it into our memories. The electronic media can broaden, deepen feelings of dislocation—sensations of alarm. Electricity pipes in multichannel communiqués and subliminal noise, the buzz of the refrigerator, the hum of the PC, the background throb of lighting, the low-frequency pulsations from heaters and air conditioners. Life breathes into our rooms: scenes and dramas spin through, with music and rumours and opinion and slow-motion highlights, paradigms of contemporary chaos and ancient myths fusing, becoming familiar and revelatory.

While those in government and in the offices of the transnationals often try to confirm renewal—the end of recessions, or depression—what people feel and identify in the humanity they see is psychic hollowing. The media quickly illuminated, in intensive beams and high subliminal frequencies, a crucial story of anxiety and fatigue. And when we observe and absorb the rulers who appear in the global theatre, scanning them through those screen irradiations, we sometimes seem to be seeing through them into data structures that have become virtually independent of their lives: the corporation itself becoming a fierce form. The rulers no longer appear to speak for themselves, and for us, but only on behalf of the structures of production.

What is the cost of being Canadian? The corporatist manifesto answers with the familiar phrases "a sound economy" and "fiscal responsibility." This is the answer obsessed with interest rates, market competitiveness—the energies of production and consumption. No individual, no people, no society or country, will find meaningful transcendence, an imaginative coring of being, if the vision is only economic. Moreover, the corporatist answer disregards a recognition of how Canada differed, and differs, from other states. It disregards questions of the good, and that deep responsiveness to our emotions and need, experiences and longings, which seeds us with the inspiration to continue and to evolve.

The transnational-corporatist shadow imposes this message: you and your country are for sale, serve anyone—or anything—that will give you the best deal, travel faster so that all things become a haze, treat all institutions (from universities to hospitals) as if they were part of the same corporation, make sure that nearly all whom you elect are prepared to be ruthless about deficit cutting, face that life is about how much you make and how much you spend but in the end find yourself dependent on the fortunes and failures of the transnationals themselves and not the self-reliant soul that economic manifestos and blueprints seemingly encourage.

Once you are prepared to do without imagination, without inspiration, and once you are prepared to dismiss talk of the value of the soul, it won't take long for those we elect and elevate to positions of power to be mesmerized by the transnational elites of privilege and influence. And then for them to convince you that your best interests will be served by obedience to the material directives, value established by the unelected and by those whose hearts have hardened. So they may lose their chance to summon our cultural myths and legacies, the spirit and concealed currents. They have lost the chance to govern bonded with the individual citizen—the one who must persevere, make sacrifices, pay the bills, dream of a better future, of a life that carries the possibility of vitality and enlightenment.

I set out to write this part in the form of a letter. It was meant to be addressed to politicians and leaders. I'd thought about singling out a prime minister, or an economic philosopher, or perhaps a minister of finance, or an IMF representative. Now I'm not sure where I would send it, and to whom. Such is the effect of the corporatist shadow. You find yourself talking to ghosts. Eventually, you begin to think in anonymous terms.

I'm also arrested by the notion that right-wing and left-wing economists share the concept that all culture is super-structure, or peripheral: what you can allow only when you have the money. I take the imagination to be the starting point of human endeavours. It must enfold economics or there will be little purpose to the amassing and distribution of wealth. Economic survivalism rapes dignity. But the answer is not more or less government—or efficient delivery services. There has to be reversal of thought, a change of heart, trans-forming the course of the money-mind to that of humane perception, the prizing of the person, and of the soul. If this became the course, then the imagination of those who rule and shape the channels of wealth would be released from their own slavery, which is servitude to mechanism—the logic of the machine, and the easy mesmerisms of the models and percentages that appear on the screens. If there is no inspiration, then the political economy becomes nothing more than heedless, insensate—a demonic reflection or parody of all the latent potencies to be found in electrodynamism.

To the corporatist-committee mind

You have misunderstood how politics and governance are about the spark in us. They are about the ways we re-envision and remould our realities. You misread the complex moods of people, reducing their strivings and fear to digits in a set of graphs. Politics is not only about fiscal restraint, it is about myths and magic. It concerns emotion and perception, how we respond to the aspiring dreams of people, what we each love, yearn for, ponder, hope for, in our higher selves. Once again I say you have cut yourselves off from the soul-root of the imagination. You blaze forward but go nowhere. You strike and enthrall and yet you don't move. Like someone incubated in a laboratory cell, your temperature regulated by the cooled purposes of the transnationals, one for whom all light must mean the snaring glares of publicity, you live submerged, unconscious, lacking in the sharp growths of the heart, disconnected from the feelings and dreams of others, the vertiginous infusions of spirit.

Now we find we must begin again to listen to the new land, this indefinable place whose elusive, and evasive, spirit still forms. Canada is the *via media*—the middle way, between the United States and Europe. We must discover that route again, and trace it, and follow, allowing its meander, attending to where its whispering path may lead.

Interlude

SECRET COUNTRY

"We can't live on poetry alone," the currency speculators say.

True: and then I reply, "Nor can we live without it."

The Trojan War without Homer was nothing more than a battle over trade routes. We need the wind and air of metaphor, of myth, or lyrical language, of verbal music, not to merely add colour and texture to our unfoldings, but to help lift our mood, and to move our souls away from the excluding focus on economic heat.

Sometimes it seems we have lost our ability to breathe and sing.

And there are fires other than those that consume us.

———————

This is where I find myself: exploring what could be heard and viewed again in the auroras of the hidden-away Canada, a secret country where solitudes and peace still largely exist, where we can ask questions about injustices and inequity, about whether there is a vocation in being Canadian, hoping against hope, expecting the impossible. Yet there is no map for this secret country because—to echo a line of Thomas Merton's—it is within our selves.

When we try to address what we take to be reality—what in fact we mean by life—it is like pointing a finger at the lights of the aurora borealis. The hand making the gesture is not important: it is the phenomenon we need to see and to comprehend. But the aurora borealis, meaning "northern dawn" or "dawn-like halo," remains visible and yet inaccessible, always slightly out of reach of our grasp. *Aurora*, the dawn, links with the Latin *aurum*, gold or golden. *Borealis*, from the Latin *boreas*, the North Wind. The essential thing is to point to the moving horizon.

Above the din we listen for music. Beyond the dimming in darkness we strive for light. This is what we must continue to do, when the auroras sometimes seem curtained off, and when the voices in the wind of this other new land seem to go quiet.

Second Meditation

ALTERNATIVE CURRENT

I was now working with that occult force, electricity, and here was a possible chance to make some discoveries . . . The early silence in a telephone circuit gave an opportunity for listening to stray electric currents that cannot be easily had today. I used to spend hours at night in the laboratory listening to many strange noises in the telephone and speculating as to their causes.

—THOMAS WATSON,
in his memoir, *Exploring Life*

Let me talk about how Canada could be a model for the first country in the post-industrial politic to be more a state in process than a nation-state.

If we reject the corporatist concept of government, its inevitable inequities and its orthodoxy of the bottom line, its economics stuck in a solution-based acceptance of linear logic, its elevation of computer programs and virtual concepts over humane and particular response, then we reject the blueprint of slash and burn, of downsizing and dehumanizing. When Canadians rejected constitutional initiatives in a referendum, we spontaneously recognized that our culture does not need to rigidly codify itself. If we begin to perceive our strengths in the story of communication, in debate and experimentation, in the resistance to violent resolution and arbitrary system, then we may say Canada is light, unburdened by constitutional weight and records of viciousness, by a militarized society or a state religion.

We can acknowledge that we follow an alternative current in the planetary city, a vision of an imaginative culture, urbane and amenable, that puts forward the higher self through reverie and solitudes. While we may sense that complete agreement is unlikely, and even undesirable, friction and contradiction our heritage, improvisation our past and present, compromise our hope, we have the opportunity to reassess the nature of political economy. In that review, which could become a revelation, we could come to see that Canada is a place, and a state of mind—still emerging, swerving away from the rule of empire, full of subjectivities, without one dominant and curbing view.

I'm not idealizing Canada. On the contrary, greed, humiliation, selfishness, arrogance, egotism are facts of the material plane. I'm not sure that these forces and moods in ourselves, and which we find in our institutions, can be legislated away. I confess to feeling ambivalent about a country that I've sometimes thought about leaving. Apathy, narrow-mindedness, timidity, inertia, repression, clubbishness and a self-satisfied censoriousness often afflict us. I could easily go on with the list of negative attributes. And I have met far too many people in Canada who slavishly emulate the business-is-everything vulgarities and rapaciousness of corporate New Yorkers or Londoners: these are the new colonial postures of people who want to travel in the borderless, often valueless, empire of capital. I hesitate, moreover, to endorse or advocate any sort of nationalism whatsoever. A cultural cosmopolitanism has always attracted me. Yet I'm a child of my country. Oscar Wilde was no doubt right when he said the muses care nothing for geography; however, perhaps the individual can't completely transcend their time and place. Over the years, I've contemplated Canada, meditating on her too, wondering what holds me here, on what keeps bringing me back to the hints of possible light. I've spent time thinking about her indigo winds. Slowly I've come to identify what I call the alternative current, an approach to governing and society, citizenship and justice, that is centred in culture, wisdom, art, science, and, above all, communication.

What is Canada?

A state in process where values may prevail over policies. A place that accepts and acknowledges pluralism and multiple perspective. Canada's erratic styles and forms, its elusiveness, even its invisibility, make it a light space. This rootlessness could be liberating: the un-housed quality, the sense of being freed from tribal membership, could be an imaginative release. A place where political leaders who take constitutional crises to be terminal points in time meet people who take them to be provisional, only sketches and traces, and not templates or blueprints, and therefore another part of the communication story. A state that values the questions that concern the qualities and characteristics of the good life above the production and powers of society. A country where there exists "Wheel within wheel," so Blake wrote in *Jerusalem*, which could modify and mediate the relentless, devouring push of transnational corporatism. A state evolving, quickly, yet cautiously, beyond structures of extremist revolution and reaction, if only we'd allow this original exploration to go on. A place where there is something sensed, lingering, tracking, persisting, hovering on the cusp of articulation, modulating almost imperceptibly, appearing in stages, gradually unveiling itself from the silence and shadows. It needs time because we need time. Ways of responding and feeling, of thinking and articulating, eventually lead to ways of living. Canada is a place whose mythology and culture speak of an incognito difference: to communicate, then to commune, with the world, rather than to conquer or subdue it. A state, then, whose very lack of a single identity, its lack of homogeneity, is its destiny.

I'll give a taste of what I mean by the alternative current in Canada through my personal experiences.

I travelled across the country for more than three years. A divorce sent me spinning. Familiar ground had dropped out from under me, and I was lost. I travelled from Toronto to Banff, to Calgary, then back to Banff and then months alone in the healing air of the Rocky Mountains. Later I went to Montreal, and on to Quebec City at Christmas, and through New Year's, and then the winter carnival time. I came back to Toronto and continued to live for a while out of a suitcase, a displaced existence. Then my life changed again when I met someone and felt once more the stirrings of reconnection, and remarried. I travelled, with her, in southern and eastern Ontario, driving to small towns and villages, beside rivers and around lakes. We left Canada for a short time, heading down to the Florida Keys, down to Key West, mile zero in North America. We came home, back to Toronto, and settled in a quiet north city neighbourhood.

In the midst of this restlessness, I often found myself musing on Canada. I'm not sure why questions about country came. But they did. Perhaps my unfixed living was like a reflection of the mutable nature of Canada. I discovered variety everywhere. I saw no evidence of empire, nothing I could say was uniformly Canadian. I never saw exaggerated displays of obstinate patriotism. Yet I sensed intangibles, subtleties that said we are unique here.

In Banff I talked to a Japanese businessman who was perplexed by the constitutional initiatives that sought to solve the Canadian puzzle. He asked, "Why try to unify a country so big, so radically different in every place I've visited? Why try to fix something that wasn't broken to begin with?"

I visited Calgary and met a businesswoman, who said, "I do business by bickering. Most of my clients live in Saskatchewan. And we're not supposed to get along. Local pride, you see. So we bicker, and gripe. We make snide remarks. And we whine. Brother, do we whine. Then we find something and make an agreement. And everyone invites the other over for dinner. We whine some more. And we celebrate. You see we'd aired all our worries through complaint."

In Quebec City I read French-language magazines and tabloids that referred only to Québécois concerns. The passionate discussion of issues and personalities in the self-referential electronic media struck me. They spoke with emotion and conviction, dissident waves of anger. Their bonds to their place were profound, and I was moved by their attachments and fascinations. While I heard people say, "Do *les anglais* truly hate us?" I did hear of pragmatic political affiliations and a long story of a tacit, understood attachment to the rest of the country.

In Westport, eastern Ontario, on the Rideau Canal System, I saw Victorian homes with hand-painted signs in windows saying, "Canada . . . Don't Give It Away . . ." People muttered cynical comments about how the government had sold out to Quebec. Yet in Westport harbour I saw houseboats from Laval, from Montreal, Cornwall and Kingston, moored side by side at the overnight dock. And in the twilight people conversed affably in fractured combinations of English and French.

In downtown Toronto I attended a biweekly discussion group, called the Committee for Debate, where entrepreneurs, consultants, politicians and writers met to argue about political reform. Although the group ultimately disbanded— in a parody of the results of constitutional conferences, no one could finally agree on much—I often heard the refrain "How can we take power from financial elites who don't have a feel for Canada?"

In Key West, by the Gulf, I talked to vacationing Americans, curious about their northern neighbour. "Is it true your country will break up and join the U.S.?" one asked. "Why would you want to do that?"

Back in Toronto, I read pundits and editorialists in newspapers who assured their readers that their country was plummeting towards dissolution. It was only a matter of time. Then I read Salman Rushdie's words in the *Toronto Star* about how

Canadians could be moral leaders: "In the same way as the Nordic countries in Europe have a long track record in human rights, Canada is, so to speak, the Scandinavia of North America."

I listened to a taxi driver, in Ottawa, who had emigrated from Mozambique. He said, "Canadians don't have troubles. Not really. You only have bellyaches."

And in the university seminars I teach, students said that "Yes" their country was elusive to them. Nevertheless, they said that they believed they were immersed in a quality of life that differed from other countries. They were adamant when they spoke of how they didn't want to be anything other than Canadian.

Late one night I stopped at a Tim Hortons donut shop on Queen Street East on my way home from downtown Toronto, and I heard night people, roughened men and women muttering about feeling cut off, about feeling lonely and powerless. I started jotting down on a napkin fragments of what they said: ". . . Government is leavin us out. Not part of what they think is okay. How can anyone get along like a corporation? Unions letting us down. Everyone lettin go. Goddamned PM. Damn difficult to hold onto a buck. Out for a job. Bangin on doors. Hittin the pavement. Any luck today? No way. Gotta hang on. Livin like my hand's out all the time. The buck passin by. Wish I could get out. Someplace other than the street. But hey they're my home y'know . . . Goddamned people know nothin. But I keep goin, gettin out . . ."

The shop was badly lit. This midnight gathering place was a replacement for a refuge. Here there was familiarity, and recognition. And there were words, even where you could feel despair—words trying to shape sense, grasp truths. I felt far away from these people. Yet I knew they too wanted to know what it means to be valued. How easy it would be to overlook these feelings of diminishment, of severing.

Through these meetings and talks and incidents and travels, I discerned a latent question about this counter-nation, its loose ties and reticent assumptions. We may have misunderstood the process we are experiencing, and we may have missed what is flourishing. By looking for constitutional guarantees and absolutes, and by allowing our politicians to turn our national debate into a question about whether we can afford or sustain Canada, we lost the implicit need and willingness to explore, sample, examine and live truly what has made each part of the country unusual. We do not lack cohesion. It comes from dialogue, and civility, the participation in differing views, our emergence through argument, counter-argument, airwaves and mixed messages, those intangibles that we know through glimmers and clues.

Canada is like several puzzles that we are all working on at the same time. Everyone has a part to add, but no one has seen the whole picture yet. So we must inevitably sway on the edge of bitter disappointment, close to failure. I found this country to be an intricate pattern with many centres, where the tensions between the individual and the collective continue in their wayward, bewilderingly risky course. And when I look over the experiences again, reviewing them, re-evaluating the patterns, I sensed a readiness, a willingness, to coexist—more: to live a difference, to turn away from destructiveness and impoverishment (of the soul) towards the full-hearted, perhaps the good, beyond what we can right now entirely perceive.

I turn to an incident I saw on Canada Day, July 1, 1992.

At that time I lived on a tree-lined street in North Toronto. The neighbourhood resembled a small town. People gathered outside their homes to talk, and gossip. They liked to talk freely, about themselves, and about what was going on in the world. Sometimes they discussed politics, and politicians, in a good-humoured, skeptical way. It wasn't hard to notice that behind the good humour and irony the future of the country mattered to them. During the spring and early summer of that year an economic gloom possessed my neighbours. And through TV, the radio, newspapers and magazines, we had all been exposed to a constitutional debate that we somehow surmised could not resolve anything: its bulky prescriptions and conclusions would not satisfy everyone.

Then on Canada Day I saw things that surprised me. I went out for a walk around the block, down the streets I thought I knew well, and in the windows of almost every home I saw the Canadian flag taped to the glass. Sometimes a small-sized flag had been set in a makeshift pole over a door, to flutter in the breeze. This was unusual. Unlike most Americans I know, with their ferocious devotion to the Stars and Stripes, most of my neighbours had admitted they weren't sure they liked the stark red-and-white design with the maple leaf stuck in the centre. Some had said they didn't much care for the flag at all. That day, when I was out strolling, I saw flags everywhere and birthday cards attached to garage doors. I saw handwritten signs wishing the country well.

Quietly, my neighbourhood expressed its hope. No one asked them to do so. In spite of the politicians and their dire warnings about the end of the country, a deep faith endured in people. I had the impression that my neighbours had recognized an essence that the rulers had overlooked, or had forgotten, or perhaps never knew, or perhaps didn't want to know.

This country's spirit lives on and thrives in the value of debate and in the tacitly understood contract that our exploring must continue.

I acknowledge a paradox in my reflections on the alternative current in Canada. The Free Trade Agreement, for all its faults, recognizes the planetary culture and its economy.

Raw data spews across borders. Strange noises scat at night online. Through computer networks transnationals can transfer their capital in one morning from Chicago to London to Zurich to Tokyo to New York City to Toronto. Electronic screens ray-gun images and words and numbers and icons into our offices and homes. Satellite dishes, radios, cellular telephones and answering machines shoot up static into our psyches. Small neighbourhoods have become nodes in this meshing of communications technologies, each street becoming abruptly like a highway for the flurry and glint of readouts. Overtones and subliminals—almost inaudible, indistinct messages on the edge of consciousness—murmur in our ears and minds. Invisible forces swirl. Energies stream past, immaterial and yet omnipresent, yanking us from our roots. This data-flux injects contradictory opinions, instant advice, entrancing fantasias, nightmare scenes of murder and ruin, paradisal moments of love, past-life recollections, auguries of the future, blatant government propaganda and tantalizing corporate advertisements, fundamentalist hot gospelling and cyberpunk manifestos of revolt.

Free trade may be a political-economic corroboration of the emerging noosphere, that electronic sound-and-sense-scape that is McLuhan's global village and Richard Maurice Bucke's "cosmic consciousness."

The accelerated pace of change makes all of our lives revolutionary. Like data addicts, we do live with our insides out, our outside wired in. Concepts of nation, nature, mind and identity become amorphous, provisional, undergoing seething redefinitions that seem at times like an electrocution of everything we once took for granted.

> When nature is eventually seen as refusing to express itself in the accepted language, the crisis explodes with the kind of violence that results from a breach of confidence. At this stage, all intellectual resources are concentrated on the search for a new language.

Thus say Ilya Prigogine and Isabelle Stengers in *Order Out of Chaos: Man's New Dialogue with Nature.* They write of their search for a comprehension of context, an awareness of the environment that we re-create and in part perceive. The irony: what I seek to describe here through language is beyond the reach of the printed word. Our culture has already metamorphosed, breakneck, into events, vicissitudes of image and sound, pictogram and vibration. Cross-border transfers of data exist without legislative fiat.

I acknowledge the paradox in my probing because I'm critical of the way our leaders and politicians have managed these transforming worlds. The rulers haven't answered the pressing questions: Whom will the state serve? Who will be the truest managers and facilitators of this racing change? What value should we affirm when trade barriers tumble, individual perspectives fracture, information swarms, political borders vanish? Who will serve to counter the corporatist interests and agenda that appear and then disappear behind those letterings IMF, GATT, NAFTA and WTO? If no one counters these seemingly impenetrable forces, then what happens to the idea of citizenship?

Absorbed in whirls of panic and of disarray, we live roused by vision, disturbed by nightmares where things appear to be run by no one we can see or identify, animated by liberating possibilities, all that must accompany the hyper-transformations. And we lack a language for the infinite connections and variations, the patterns that unravel and unfold. So we step hesitantly, sometimes awkwardly, or reluctantly, into abysses, unsure that there will be anything solid beneath us. Every day brings upset and invitations to risk whatever consistency and definition we may have known. Intimate with the rolling and unrolling effects of mass technology, the waves, we nevertheless don't always know how to precisely describe how machines mimic us (through simulation), encourage us to long for signs of ancestry (so uprooted we hunt for tokens of the past, vestiges of family history, precedents in records and chronicles, revivals of ethnic lineage), exaggerate our foibles (people on screens becoming grotesques and cartoons) and converge (corporations move to meld all aspects of communications, dissolving more lines between private life and work). What were once the wilderness trials and baptisms of adepts and wandering mystics, of bohemian poets and visionaries keen to deliberately dislocate their senses, are now our transactions and preparations, everyday spectacle. We overdose on electricity, the force fields of the universe, through TV, radio, microwaves, fax machines, cellulars and computers, and, acute receivers that we are, we reel—cranked, battered, boosted, infinitely suggestible.

When we join TV and radio and the computer and the telephone with the old non-electric print technologies of the book and the newspaper, we could learn to become adept at reading the presence, and maybe the essence, of those we elevate and elect. We may be able to make transparent those who want to withdraw behind the sphinx-like acronyms and abbreviations of the transnationals. Eyewitnesses, ear-witnesses, playing the ensemble of instruments, using the moments we have to become poet-seers. These inventions not only extend our faculties into space and time, thus sometimes wrenching our minds and searing our senses, but at the same time they help to restore insight into the mass sheen and wail of the teleworld. Replay, freeze-frame, slow-motion, fast-forward, image enhancement, storage and retrieval, sampling and editing, Internet interpretations and more interpretations, are part of the global language that could galvanize us into charting and humanizing those who disappear behind powerful abstract corporate masks or who appear flittingly on our screens, and speak to us from radio-bands, trying to direct us, making their pitches, uttering their clichés, attempting to lead or to block us.

Allow me to imagine what the alternative current could mean for Canada. I'd like to dream of a new pattern that joins thinking and intuition, another way of working and perceiving, a changed apprehension of political process and the effects that politicians can have on the moods and actions of others.

What is Canada? A place without aggressive nationalisms. Canadians could be a people who recognize that our country is a state in process rather than a conventional nation with one goal or direction, whether that goal is called "fiscal responsibility" or "security." It could be a state, a condition, where questions of human value (rights' debates), where ambiguity, privacies, the multilinguistic dialogues and translations, are allowed to become habits of mind. Our resistance to any effort to impose or obtrude meaning through constitutional fiat can be a sign of spiritual patience and vigour.

The mistake for us is to see ruin in confusion and chaos. I observed earlier that the corporatist manifesto, the Wilson blueprint, was a bottom-line template for an economy that had once been an arrangement of public- and private-sector alliances. That agenda sought to reconfigure Canada into a stock-exchange commodity. Some of the corporatist questions were good ones: How do we restructure our economy to best serve people? How do we create and channel wealth? However, the concern for deficit reduction soon led to the monomania about numbers and percentages. The rulers recognized the social and financial turbulence of what came to be called globalization: their answer was callous and unimaginative.

When Joanne Kelleher interviewed Tom Peters—of *In Search of Excellence* fame—in *Computerland* (March 8, 1993), she asked, "What should IBM do to fix itself?" Peters replied, "Prayer would be my strongest suggestion." His apparently flippant response is not far off from the Delphic maxim "Know yourself." Explore and question your motives and methods of proceeding: recognize strands of association. Each of us is matter to be shaped, dust to be breathed into and gathered up. Find out what is the best and the worst in you: transmute and transcend those energies, if you can. Look for guidance. But the mediating imagination, our link to the soul, holds the key.

The corporatist blueprint posed questions about wasted wealth. These problems must be addressed by the elected, the governors. But there must be paths we can take without provoking even more panic and fear. If we shifted our thinking, our states of perception to conceive of another model, with different premises—acknowledging the seeds in the self—then our attention could be drawn to inventive action.

Let us fully imagine the stateless state where politics is not driven by fanatics, factionalism or violence, by inflexible ideologies and fundamentalist dogmas, where the cultures of the world can and do exist together. There are many languages in

Canada, not just the official three: there are many cultures, not a homogenous one. The danger in this myriad-minded approach is lasting divisiveness, more isolation. The Canadian pattern and response could splinter into fragments—provincial shards that will never cohere. The polyphony of voices could flip into an aimless jumble—an oppressive babble. Improvisation could become a desperate groping after a main theme. This country's paradoxes could become irreconcilable polarities. Ethnic groups could circle around themselves, excluding others, accusing one another of intrusions and violations, nursing old wounds.

But if we recall the summoning and announcement of the new in the symbol of the CN Tower—a spire and medium whose essential use is the reception and transmission of multiple messages—then we could hold on to the feel for this antenna culture, the responsive and reflective zone of a North American visionary intelligence. The tower spirals upwards, and tells us, always, "Look up."

Third Meditation

TOWARDS A CANADA OF LIGHT

Here is a sphere or change, change, change.
Through change consume change.

—From a transcription
of ancient Sanskrit manuscripts

Quebec City, February 1991.

It was there that I began to think about my country's enigmas, and how its variety and frictions could be its enduring qualities.

I lived briefly inside the old city's walls. The corporatist state of mind seemed to be reaching some zenith: the government's financial and constitutional policies had become dramatically apparent. For the first time in my travels across Canada I did begin to wonder if our federation would be eventually absorbed into a uniform North American trade bloc.

One morning I walked along rue St-Denis, down to the Dufferin Terrace at the foot of the sloping street. Cold air swept in off the frozen St. Lawrence. Blue sky and fresh snow from the evening before. Icy winds made the turrets, sooted spires, blackened chimneys and slanted roofs look sharp-edged in a white light. I looked closely at the winding cobbled streets and the antique buildings of *la Basse-Ville* to the south and the steel-sheeted business towers to the west.

The winter can come down hard here, like a thick, pearl curtain. And it can come down like a cloud of down feathers. Winter can oppress, beating everyone almost senseless with its battery of cold. And it can refine the air in a bracing rite of purification. It can make everything feel hard and angular— abrasively jagged with marshalled ice pellets. And it can soften streets and slow into quaintness this huddled city that still preserves the romance of the old. The glittering blue and crystalline light brings a peculiar exotic feel to the season. Townspeople ski into work and to shops; at night you hear the clip-clop and Christmas jangle of horses with their weight of sleighs and carriages. Your senses are heightened—though the cold can drug you into a stupor that prevents you from realizing that frostbite is only a moment away, snapping easily at exposed hands and faces.

Nowhere else in my country would I see such an abrupt, beautiful contrast of the old world and the new. An image of harmony: there was the small scale of the town, lanes measured and meandering, designed for walking and pausing: and the mirror-shade city, elevators and escalators rising and falling inside the towering shapes. The traditional lower streets, with their evocation of repose, a slower way of living, complemented the trim, cool, rectilinear buildings, and their impression of idling machines, poised for high-speed escape from the earth's gravity.

It came to me that what the rulers took to be cynicism in citizens was glaring, dislocating fear. The forces of fear had temporarily won in Canada. Anxiety seeped inside everyone, into the atmosphere of our time. How could you identify it? You could almost touch the worry, the weariness, the mistrust and the recoil in people's lives. It was the most primary and stark of feelings: the naked fear that seldom left most people and could be used to keep them in such a state of panic and terror that they would not act, that they could be convinced to believe anything in the name of security.

What brought about the fear? Where could you find its origins?

You could find dread and alarm latent in the systems of thought that used the language of downsizing and credit ratings to determine human value. You could see it in the words that meant people would be sent whirling without a promise of relief—structures that meant wealth and privilege and knowledge and purpose would be concentrated in the hands of the few, so that only the most ruthless would be celebrated. The rulers weren't ignorant, incompetent governors: they were bright-eyed zealots, persuaded of their righteous mission. They spoke in codes of the final answer, of absolutes, of enemies of prosperity, of exclusive access to information. In the formulae uttered about restraints and cuts came the politics of elimination and polarization. Survival-of-the-Fittest capitalism was back. After a time of imaginative political exercise in the 1960s and early 1970s—furious times that often squandered financial resources—the opposing power had shadowed up in society, and finally in government. This was the fearful force that found expression in shutdowns, limitation, pink slips, efficient management. It was the force of thought that said, between the lines, "Canada doesn't really exist . . . We can't afford this country so let's make the best deal possible . . . We know what's best for you . . . Originality and daring must be sacrificed to the debt . . . Accept the borders of the reality we will set for you . . ."

I stood there, on the terrace, overlooking the iced surface of the river. Wind blew up snowdrifts and carved white dunes.

Suddenly I realized that forces of fear had hauled in their spiritual baggage of accusation and paranoia. The cold climate needed warm souls. But the mood of my country seemed to rapidly become one where people shrugged off the rulers, mumbling, "That's just them doing things to us again . . . ramming things down our throats . . ."

The forces of fear had brought their victory with hardened hearts, deafened ears, blunted sensitivities, exhausted spirits, dimmed imaginations. In this numbness began irresponsibilities. Their success could only lead to belief in necessity and will, in an excessive greed itself. And though I knew that will, and necessity, and indeed rage and even a portion of greed, can be essential to the soul's growth, these factors left out transcendent vision, wise foundations—the pursuit of knowing, of truth. They left out compassion, and what was once called the good.

Standing there on the Dufferin Terrace, I looked behind me, back at the Château Frontenac, the small park, the small row homes and the American Consulate. Then I turned and gazed down at *la Basse-Ville*.

I imagined something else then: how lost we were becoming while we made our journey into the cyclotrons of international finance and mobile currencies. I realized we were experiencing the loss of a frame of reference, or ways of looking at colliding worlds. We'd lost a tenor of life to which we'd grown accustomed. This was leading to frayed nerves, whiplashes of anger. Canada could be ripped apart by that hyper-intensity of telecommunications. We suffered from a surfeit of discrete interpretations, apparently disconnected bits. Such whirlwinds provoke paranoia. The corporatist years in government had become a time of suspicion, of near hopelessness—the fear was immense, and overmastering.

Something seemed to be fading in my country. I'd felt the slipping away in my life, and during my stay in Quebec City.

Yet I thought that value and purpose would be found again in Canada. Even when I was away, I couldn't escape the feeling that a sounding of meaning, a pressing towards the heart, was underway. Whatever it was that was happening was pivotal: a global story, finding crystallized form in a drama. The enigmas of place and time kept drawing me home.

I thought of Canada, this place seemingly on the verge of losing its way. I'd observed the impact of overload in the harshness of conflicting opinions—in the steeling of positions. I saw how many people had lost direction in their lives. I'd witnessed how leaders in almost every political party, in almost every government, were leaving a bequest of delusions about eliminating deficits, a legacy that was solidifying into a stringent, absolutist approach to economics. It was becoming clearer that the force of mind that saw things purely in terms of the bottom line ruled every decision, every angle. No other concern seemed to enter the rulers: the result was the obsession with power.

Loss preyed on us. And for some people our country no longer appeared to expand towards a Canada of light and air and wind and free space, a big land welcoming spirits and fresh imaginings.

Where were we to start again?

If we were to be discoverers, we had to engage and re-imagine our perceptions of the communications fields and their hyper-transformations. It was unlikely that anyone could escape the barrages and radical diffusions of data, the sensory stimulations and virtual simulations of the wired-in pulse. I knew there was a lot to learn about what it means to be hooked up: how an individual could be contemplative and absorbed, moved and detached, implicated and observant, pliant and rebellious. There was more to be learned, more to be said, about this secret country, and its contradictory moods.

Later when I returned to Toronto I began to think about the meaning of the phrase "Towards a Canada of Light." It came back to me, lingering. I walked around the city—loving those long walks into every part of Toronto—and reflected on its wild urban sprawl and the ambitions of the architects of the high-towers downtown. Sometimes I carried books with me, works by Václav Havel, and by Blake. In Havel's essay "Paradise Lost," I read this passage on the political process

> Those who find themselves in politics therefore bear a heightened responsibility for the moral state of society, and it is their responsibility to seek out the best in that society, to develop it and strengthen it . . .

I saw the rulers in the corporatist mould had spoken to the worst in us. They'd addressed the shadow of force, the fear that drives people into the need to belong to larger protectorates and systems. They had incited the extreme polarizations of wealth and had helped, through their clichés and platitudes, to dull and inhibit our imaginative volition and reach.

I put Havel's sentences together in my mind with an insight I remembered from Robert Pirsig's *Zen and the Art of Motorcycle Maintenance*

> If a revolution destroys a systematic government, but the systematic patterns of thought that produced that government are left intact, then those patterns will repeat themselves in the succeeding government.

Pirsig's epiphany illuminated for me the cycles of entrapment and oppression that Blake had mythologized in his epics and lyrics. At last I read and understood his lines where he stated the visionary intent to break those confining cycles, the darker states of mind, limiting mechanisms of thought: to inspire us to become creator-citizens who are

> Striving with Systems to deliver
> individuals
> from those Systems . . .

Look into your souls, these poets and philosophers exhorted: know what you are, school your inwardness: know what the world means to you, what you want the world to be. If you want to know how power moves, how ideology and systems and prejudices and plans, in fact tyranny itself, can beguile and enmesh those who are in government, and those who run the transnationals, then understand your ambitions and needs, motives and actions. Like man, like state. To put this baldly: man is his state.

To break with these cycles and their hard economic policies will take brave, inventive people. But Canada has always been an intangible, difficult place. We persist in perceiving the traces, the lineaments of the alternative current, and the aspirations of higher selves, another way of imagining our state so that somewhere moral courage and the reality of the dream of a full life, of mediation and experimentation, will thrive.

An enlightened state would have to exist more lightly than a nation bloated by constitutional restrictions, the administrations of an empire, borders and colonies and satellites and protectorates to police with a military establishment and a National Security Council. Such a state would be an evolutionary civilization rather than a revolutionary society.

> . . . real peace . . . must always rest upon a peace of mind; whereas the so-called armed peace, as it now exists in all countries, is the absence of peace of mind. One trusts neither oneself nor one's neighbours, and, half from hatred, half from fear, does not lay down arms. Rather perish than hate and fear, and twice rather perish than make oneself hated and feared—this must some day become the highest maxim for every single commonwealth.

"Rather perish than hate and fear . . ." Unexpected words from Friedrich Nietzsche and *The Will to Power*. They speak to the promise of a country like Canada, or to the Canada we could carry inside us.

By a light state I don't mean a political, social Utopia.

Josef Skvorecky may write in *The Engineer of Human Souls*, through the eyes of his central character, Daniel Smiricky

> . . . The Toronto skyline is more beautiful to me than the familiar silhouette of Prague Castle. There is beauty everywhere on earth, but there is greater beauty in those places where one feels that sense of age which comes from no longer having to put off one's dreams until some improbable future. . . .

Every place has its furies, its turmoil, its inequities, its horrors. Experimental heavens launched through social engineering have a habit of turning into hells. There is a share of intolerance, brutality, stupidity and guilt in Canada—in the treatment of the Aboriginal peoples, the battles of the Northwest Rebellion, in the Winnipeg riots on Bloody Saturday in June 1919, in the devastating internment of Japanese Canadians during World War II, in the often unsparing and indiscriminate application of the War Measures Act in 1970—there is degradation for the homeless who tramp city streets, a humiliating entrapment and frustration for people who live under the poverty line, unfairness and abuse in businesses, schools, churches and homes. No state must ever be an end in itself. I do, however, sense the potential for another kind of relationship here between citizen and government, culture, and communications.

Moreover, I believe the prospects of paradise must persist in us. We feel its absence: we reflect on its sway, its magnetic pull: we dismiss it, and demonize it: we call it unattainable, unreal, and yet how we long for its gifts, its abundance. Our every political, social aspiration, our yearnings for warmth and kindness desperately recall it, and conjure it. Any idea or design of a country that does not include at least the possibility of paradise is not a design worth believing in or extolling.

Leave Canada to her lightness.

Let us tell whomever comes to power to let our country be light, not weighted down by eighteenth- and nineteenth-century concepts of nationhood, narrowing grids and templates, the formal apparatus of a homogenizing economic system and legislation that attempt once and for all to resolve the disparate elements and paradoxes that make up this society. Leave her to her ambivalences, her evasions, her frictions, her civility, her elusiveness, her patient unfolding: leave her to the debates, the haggling and wheedling and complaining and coaxing. Meaning resides for us in the ways that we address injustices, in the dialogues we support, in the messages that are sent and received, in the discontinuities between the regions, in the rendezvous of cultures, in what we intuit about our secret selves.

A digital simulation in a computer works through a pattern of light, a pattern of shadows. One makes the imaginative leap: every person reflects and emanates their own light and shadow, a free-floating side to their personality and a tragic, murderous, power-hungry dimension. We send our darkness and light into the world. The electronic media amplify this darkness and light to the point of apocalyptic intensity.

The Canadian shadow often appears to us in the projected shape of a looming prospect of assimilation into the United States, and its burdened history. The other shadow is the overbearing atmosphere of fear.

Whatever we allow to grow in Canada should continue without warnings and threats from politicians about an imminent national Judgment Day. Then what unfolds here could be original, rich, quietly audacious, full of eccentricities, respectful of the enigmas of difference. Evolution over revolution, metamorphosis over Armageddon—these could be our credos. An overly formulated and detailed constitution is a recipe for fanaticism. Let us sustain our native irony for all things official, absolutist, imposed and unitary. Rather than look for political unity—an ultimately futile question and pursuit—let us look for harmony, the deeper arrangement and cohesiveness of contraries. Let us welcome what is multiform, flexible, personalized, paradoxical, unwonted, curious and protean.

What will connect us? What gives us vision and voice?

Venture this: under the official news, the editorials and opinions, the corporate propaganda and the prepared speeches of many rulers, and the mind's chatter that comes from the noise of our media daze, people sense a spirit and motion not yet articulated, still felt, one possessed by inklings, or premonitions, of hope and evolution. They are only inklings, a mere breath; but that may be enough. When a government or transnational turns its citizens or workers into objects, digits, data and decimal points, then people will begin to feel acutely, painfully, human in their estrangement. Alienation and loneliness plant the seeds for rebellion and consciousness. What systems, polls, financial templates and corporate strategies deny is the aspiring individual, the root of purpose and value. Systems push things downward: their method is one that imposes structure, attempts to freeze meaning. It is the individual who must learn how to rise up, choose, interpret and love. Paradoxically, the severe bottom-line approach to the economy—programmed by people whose responsibility and compassion, foresight and generosity we question—may inspire the vital counter-agency: the hunger to retrieve the integer of the soul.

Politicians and transnational leaders have tapped into economic, electronic, social, psychological and psychic energies that they don't understand. They did not foresee the effects of what they glibly called an adjustment, a revaluing of wealth.

The Russian philosopher and dissident Alexander Herzen, in *From the Other Shore*, an essay he wrote more than one hundred years ago, said this about such engineering

> If progress is the goal, for whom are we working? Who is this Moloch who, as the toilers approach him, instead of rewarding them, draws back . . . a goal which is infinitely remote is no goal, only . . . a deception; a goal must be closer—at the very least the labourer's wage, or pleasure in work performed.

May each election and referendum continue to shake us to our roots. In those paroxysms—our civil replacements for wars and revolutions—we may find out what our country is made of and what thought and dreams we want to encourage.

Envision a place that preserves the capacity to respond, where sensibilities have not been stunted by too much power, comfort, conventional thinking or wealth, or by despair, inertia, terror or poverty, where minds haven't been thoroughly propagandized by a singular theoretical approach. Envision a country where inwardness, the life of imagination, of conscience, of sympathy and concern, can prosper in tacit, subtle resistances. Imagine a place fit for dreaming. Canada's raison d'être is a slower rhythm, punctuated by those sudden outbreaks called elections and referenda that incite and inspire questioning and interpretation, the discovery of links, the revelation of character. Without a compelling case for cultural meanings—the kind we find in the communication stories—then everything becomes an economic arrangement, a soulless politics of deals. Envision a country: ours, here, still evolving.

We will need politicians who are more than mere handlers and facilitators of power and deals. We need counter-politicians, who can contemplate and advocate our country's profound ambiguities and ambivalences. It's good for the rulers to be constantly challenged: referenda and elections, Internet gatherings and probes, put them on notice. And what will citizens need? Patience, and more patience, the time to learn and to disagree, to recognize the implicit pattern of contraries at play, the time to prepare to resist and defy those who encode fear.

If we could see in confusion and hear in the noise the new structures of consciousness emerging, then we might say that the communication state could become our identity, our offering to the world.

If we could see that our light state may in fact be a condition of receptivity, of living without borderlines, of trust and the willingness to talk and to debate, then we might say that breakdown is part of the process, setback can be a kind of gift, and we may then step back from cataclysmic finale and gloom, and the rapacity of consumption and greed. We might acknowledge that the nation-state is disappearing, and the new model is decentralized, mythic, planetary and complex.

If we could see that we can't stop the attractions and repulsions of electricity, that our technologies magnify the effects of electromagnetism on us, then we could see that we are moving into a world embrace, a deeper and quicker enfolding of lives and events.

If we could see that through multimedia convergence we recognize ourselves, engaging the human conundrum and situation, *existenz* in incessant feedback, in ways that couldn't have been conceived decades ago (a circumstance resembling the first time people saw themselves in the gloss of mirrors, not realizing how reflecting glass can distort, exaggerate, reveal and flatter, all while showing how you look from a reversed perspective), then we might say that some honed awareness stirs, and that our lives are now inherently, radically visionary.

If we could see how electronic eyes and ears confer clairvoyance and clairaudience on everyone who wears and uses the instruments available, then we might understand the exhilaration and terror that must follow our visionary present.

If we could see that our state is built from variety, not uniformity, and that unity must always be implicit, more a matter of harmonies, and not explicit, then we might say that we are moving towards a tremendous imagined space of light and air, with grounding in questions of justice.

If we could see that most people share the hunger for justice, for pondering and grasping what it means to have a life of quality, then the fear that accompanies the *accelerando* of technological change could be transformed into an influx of intuitions, thoughts, resources and needs.

If our dreams can last, then we could turn our time and place to gold.

Why are we here?

To be new, to make a difference, in the wilderness of power and pain, in the arenas of exploitation and humiliation. This process of engagement can exalt and exhilarate us. We may not be able to prevent suffering or degradation—we may not be able to stop the insufferable arrogance and insensitivity of those who purport to lead us—but we may be able to make all of this less the case.

So we must be tough visionaries, keen and reasonable, daring tragedy, aware of our propensities for apathy, ignorance, avarice and savagery. Then we may say that Canada's hidden destiny is to follow a path that diverges from egotism and violence, and to build a place where people could say, "All the forces and contradictions, the qualities and contrasts of our souls exist here side by side." Maybe then we will be able to wholly imagine the alternative current, perceive that we are evolving a state without walls and comprehend how we are pioneering a society whose communication stories express the myths of receptivity and constant negotiation, the anonymous place, the many-sided state, the pluralistic country without a single identity. Then we may sense in the hints and static that we hear over the airwaves that Canada's very impossibility is her hope and her possibility.

Coda

May the ability to see many points of view keep us gentle.

May the ability to see a future keep us bold.

May the ability to recognize and reject hard-headed inequities and needless cruelties keep us compassionate and hopeful.

May the ability to perceive patterns that are yet to be fully realized keep us directed in our hearts and minds.

May your heart be touched, don't let it shrivel or let its beat be diminished: let your heart go unprotected.

May you know how to reposition yourself, and keep the compass of your heart under the stars.

May the ability to communicate and to face facts, and yet to dream new dreams and to imagine fuller lives, give us the sweet strength we need.